Alpha Male

Alpha Male Bible:

Become Legendary,

A Lion Among Sheep

Jack Landry

Table of Contents

INTRODUCTION

I sense that you're probably not content with who you are as a man. Maybe deep inside, you feel who you are right now is what you were destined to be. Maybe you want more out of life in terms of experiencing success in your career and relationships. I don't blame you. You only get one shot at life so you should indeed make the most out of it. And that requires success in most if not all areas of your life.

Being a bold person is not reserved for others. That thinking is gone. For a short time, park any of those thoughts. Bracket them. You can pick them up later if you want them but for now suspend judgment. Open your mind to the possibility that you are an alpha. You may be unsure about some things. You may question your ability to be a charismatic person, a bold leader or a magnet for people (ok, women). I wrote this book just for you. I know what it's like to have moments of questioning yourself. The secret is, you are a perfect alpha. You don't need anything else in order to be ready; everything is within you. This book is simply about taking off the layers of protection and self-doubt you have built over the years. Trust me; you will feel so free being the authentic self you have in there. That alpha is there.

Such success requires many different things. However, there's one common thread that ties all such successes together, particularly for us men. It's being an alpha male — being a lion among sheep.

I used to be a sheep, too. No, not literally in my past life, but figuratively as a man. But some life experiences, particularly painful failures with women drove me to seriously change who I am. Initially, I just wanted to be really good with women. But after learning the principles of being an alpha male and successfully applying them to women, I found that it's also applicable to other equally important areas of my life, including my career. I don't want you to go through what I went through. Take my lessons and use my insights. See what fits for you. Most men I have worked with are somewhat afraid to embrace the alpha they feel inside. Do not fall into this trap. Do not deny yourself a life that blows your mind. You deserve it. If you have a hard time believing you deserve it, do read on. Don't let yourself get stuck in a life that is okay but not great. You only have this life. Even throwing away today being a lamb is a waste of your potential. I believe in you. Join my thinking for a short time and give yourself a new lease on life.

In this book, I'll share with you those important lessons that helped transform me from a sheep to a lion – into an alpha male. If I was able to do it, so can you. You can be a lion – an alpha. I'll also share how to embrace your inner lion. Further, I'll give you some great, relatable examples that may inspire you.

Enough of small talk. Let's hit the ground running and start your crash course on becoming legendary lion among sheep.

Jack Landry

CHAPTER 1

INTRODUCTION TO THE ALPHA MALE

One common denominator of super-affluent alpha men is the conviction, unchallenged every day, that the world revolves around them. ~Tina Brown

Alpha is the Greek alphabet's first letter and it the same numeric system, it's assigned the value "1". In today's modern language, alpha refers to top person:

-At the top of the social chain;

-The boss;

-The most powerful;

-The strongest;

-The supreme; or

-The ultimate.

When it comes to being the man, alpha males are the top dogs. What does this mean? An alpha male is one who is the most dominant in a group or assumes a domineering or dominant part in professional or social situations. He's the king.

In the basketball world, LeBron James is alpha. In the bodybuilding scene, Phil Heath is alpha. In football or soccer, it's Cristiano Ronaldo who's the alpha – at least in 2014. In tennis, Novak Djokovic is the alpha male.

"Some guys have all the luck, some guys have all the pain, some guys get all the breaks, some guys do nothing but complain." Rod Stewart

You don't need to be the best or top in the world to be alpha. In fact, when it comes to being an alpha male, it's all about personality and not rankings. It just so happens that those men who I mentioned to be on top of their game happen to be the best in the world in terms of ranking. But the reason they're alpha is because of what got them there.

One of the common misconceptions about human alpha males is that they're very much like their animal counterparts. Nothing could be farther from the truth! Maybe that's why many omega (last) males are hesitant to become alpha males or shudder at the thought of becoming one – they fear becoming less human and more animal.

Truth is, animal alpha males behave differently from their human counterparts. Take two species where the concept of alpha males is very prominent – wolves and primates. Among wolves, there's actually a hierarchy that every member of the pack is expected to follow. Among primates, in particular baboons, the alpha dominates his group of lackeys or subordinates only until someone else challenges and overthrows him. In both species, alpha males are all about exerting more brute power.

What, or who exactly is an alpha male? A tall, dark, handsome man in a bar, silently nursing his drink? Or a tough, rugged-looking guy in cowboy boots and dirty jeans, with a cigarette dangling from his mouth? Or a strong, silent man who will rise to the occasion and defend his mate's honor? Who is this creature? Simply put, an alpha male is the highest-ranking individual who is designated so due to certain qualities or traits that he possesses. This is true in the case of animals as well as human beings. Not just males, females can also be designated as the alpha female.

As a general rule, the alpha animals command respect and preferential treatment from their followers or other members of the pack or group. They gain easier access to people, things, power, security, and stability, etc. Other animals in the pack or other people in the group usually defer to them. These alpha animals or males attain their superior status through their physically imposing and mentally tough characteristics, notably aggression, dominance, and control. They are equally strong in forging alliances within their groups and among other groups. Now, one single animal or person does not hold the position of the alpha for a long period of time. Clashes between the members, fights, and similar circumstances change the power play and a new alpha emerges.

The second in-command animals or members of a group are known as beta. They are only a few rungs below the alpha and they offer a serious threat to the authority of the alpha, at times. They usually emerge as the new alphas when the reigning alpha goes down for some reason. For example, in the case of wolves, when an alpha wolf dies, the beta wolf will soon take its place and mate with the females.

The lowest rung in the hierarchy is occupied by the omegas. They are usually the most obedient animals or people in the group. Due to their submissive nature, they are almost always expected to remain subservient and compliant to the alphas and betas. Their guile frequently leads them to be used as communal scapegoats. Given their low social status, omegas are the last ones to receive food, shelter, water, power, and status.

Take the case of gorillas. The huge, scary-looking, hairy apes intimidate and bully their way into the alpha circle. A study was conducted on the reproductive behavior of male mountain gorillas. It was found that the males who were dominant or stronger were more favored by the females to mate with, even when there were other males in the vicinity. The study also discovered that, given the choice between alpha, beta, and omega males, the females always went with the alpha males.

Long before humans evolved on this planet, alpha males have been in existence. Be it mammals, reptiles, birds, fish, take any species; the alpha male has continually upped the ante and has got everything he wanted. The best chicks (literally and figuratively), the most power, spectacular success, respect, and other fringe benefits of heading the pack. This is not a recent phenomenon. It goes back millions of years ago. While the alpha male got the choicest of picks, other males stood by and bowed to him. Women flocked to the alpha male in droves, side stepping the nice and sweet guys. This begs the question: why? Why does this happen? Who is this alpha male? Why do women not care for the nice guys and head straight toward the macho guy? Why does the alpha male get the best of everything?

Look at any close-knit group or a pack of animals. There is always a leader, a lone entity who shoulders maximum responsibility, who holds major assets, is dominating and powerful, and serves as a support structure for the entire group. This is the alpha male. He is the ultimate boss, whose word is law. But don't be fooled by the image of the alpha male. While some of them do utilize their superior status to browbeat those inferior to them, or persecute them unnecessarily, if only to show their haughty side, some of the alpha males play it to their advantage. They realize the effect of their natural charm and sweetness on others and capitalize on it completely to win others over and keep them under their thumb, thus protecting their turf and keeping a firm check on their reign.

So, what makes an alpha male "alpha?" Does he have a macho gene? Turns out, the answer is testosterone, the male hormone. If we look back in history, early man depended largely on what he could kill and bring home as food for his family. This act could either catapult him into the alpha league or throw him down the ladder. The man who could kill the largest animal, or wield the heaviest weapon, or pull and push the biggest boulders, and also father an enormous brood of children was the ultimate alpha male. It's simple proportion. The higher the testosterone levels, the higher the virility, the higher the sex drive, the higher the muscle mass, and in proportion, the higher the number of females flocking toward the alpha male. Nice guys be damned. Women have always wanted a testosterone-charged male to mate with, thus ensuring healthy offspring and protection.

That was then. If an early man wanted to be the alpha male of the pack, all he had to do was build a good-sized body by lugging and lifting heavy things, hunting the best animals for food, sowing his seed far and wide, grunting, and looking macho. In today's times, the poor males cannot hunt without the EPA and ten other environmental agencies breathing down their necks. No more tackling wild animals, displaying their heads over the dining room table or showing off their virility by depositing their genetic material everywhere. But modern man sure has overcome these hurdles with aplomb.

We humans aren't like that at all. We're much more, shall we say, complicated. For one, we're more social than apes and dogs, i.e., we belong to several different social circles at the same time, e.g., office, family, golfing buddies, hobby groups, etc. For example, we may be a bookkeeper by day but an underground rock star by night. Or we can be tough cops on the beat by day and, when we come home, we're the most loving and cheerful dads to our kids.

So when we speak of alpha males as humans, what we're actually talking about is a social dominance trait and not a physical one. Proof of this is that there are a lot of men in prisons. Go figure. Others hold such social dominance in high esteem in society; women are attracted to it while non-alpha males cower at it.

MAN VS. WILD

Now you see that, although the human concept of alpha male is similar to animals' in the sense of being dominant, ours is more social than physical. In the remaining chapters we'll look at the other characteristics both physical and social that you can change or influence to your favor to help turn you into an alpha male.

As we get right into the nitty-gritty of how to become a lion among the sheep, allow me to end this chapter with a quote from Miranda Hart: "It's a real man who can go out with a woman who's taller than he is. That's an alpha male right there."

Jack Landry

CHAPTER 2

AT HOME WITH SELF

A great figure or physique is nice, but it's self-confidence that makes someone really sexy. ~Vivica A. Fox

The alpha male is a man who has no problems being with himself. It may sound very simple and we may even think that it's easy to be ourselves all the time but the truth is, it isn't. If it was, then why are many men uncomfortable with themselves? The fact that you're reading this e-book probably means you, too, are having a difficult time being comfortable in your own skin.

The single biggest reason why many men aren't able to enjoy such freedom and emotional security is because they don't live with authenticity of who they really are. In other words, they aren't able to live from their core being. Notice that being true to yourself isn't something that'll necessarily make you a more socially responsible person or will help you make the world a much better place. Doing so, together with knowing how to love yourself, are the ways to experience joy in life. If you don't live from your core values and beliefs and instead live according to other people's core values and beliefs, believe me – you'll just end up living a life of pure misery. And misery doesn't make for an alpha male.

Believe it or not, all of us began our lives living it as authentic as we can within our abilities. Sadly, society has beaten the crap out of our authentic living with so many expectations and psychological conditionings in the form of rules, regulations, punishments, rewards, and life experiences. While etiquette and polite manners are important for a functioning society, somewhere along the line we've been led to believe it as an all-encompassing principle – that it's bad to be ourselves when with others! Or, how about the very popular kind of social pressure based on the saying that first impressions last and that it would do us well to not be ourselves and act in ways that society will most favorably look upon. I call it the people-pleasing disease.

One such conditioning is that it pays to be "nice" boys as a way of getting to the top. I haven't met a successful man at the top of his game who's shy, bashful, or too prim and proper. No, being shy, bashful, and too prim and proper can actually spell the death of one's career. There needs to be a level of social dominance characteristics running in one's veins if there's any hope of making it at the top. For that to happen, one must first live authentically and be really comfortable under their own skin.

HOW TO BE FREE UNDER YOUR OWN HIDE

Next time that you feel like doing something you really don't want to do or saying something you really don't want to say, mentally scream "Not me!" in your head and simply don't! It's simple but not easy and it may take quite a while to get used to, especially if you've lived your life mostly trying to please others and haven't developed the backbone to stand up for yourself just yet. Consider this a social muscle and as with physical muscles, regular exercise strengthens it over time.

One thing that can help you break the bondage of people-pleasing and living an authentic life that makes you comfortable under your own skin is by analyzing what you're getting out of people-pleasing and what you're missing out on by not being true to your core. Chances are, there are more negatives than positives and therefore, this —against your expectations—exercise can help you become more authentic faster.

For those situations where pleasing people seems to realistically be more beneficial than being authentic, try incorporating more of yourself into it to make it more comfortable for you. Take, for example, family dinners. My parents can be quite assertive when it comes to these and in most instances, I'd rather skip them. But knowing it's important for family relationships, I would incorporate some of my "core being" into it by asking them that we have some of our family dinners at my chosen restaurant.

Giving up people-pleasing also can mean that you accept yourself enough to accept other's judgment. Their judgment becomes about them and not about you. When you fully accept yourself and live authentic to you, it does not bother you that someone does not approve of your decision. The fact is, there are constant demands on us from other people – our families, our partners, our bosses, our friends and so on. Other people see the world a certain way, and if they could have it their way, you would be a certain thing or do a certain thing. As you know, sometimes what other people want does not always align with what feels right for us. It doesn't always align with what we want. This is where you can exercise your alpha skills. Practice following your gut or intuition. Practice honoring you and being authentic to you.

Sometimes people think of intuition as a fluffy thing. If you talk to a neuroscientist or a psychologist, however, you will understand intuition in a whole new way. In an article published in Psychology Today in 2014, entitled "The Science Behind Intuition" Dr. Kelly Turner described that our quick processing mechanism in the brain (also called intuitive decision-making) can be effective in many ways: "...other studies have found that, when it comes to making major life decisions, such as which house to buy or which person to marry, trusting your intuition leads to better outcomes than trusting your logical, thinking brain. In one such study ["On making the right choice: the deliberation-without-attention effect", Dijksterhuis et al., published in Science, 2006], car buyers who had plenty of time to pour over all of the information about their various car choices were later found to be satisfied with their purchase only 25% of the time. Meanwhile, those buyers who made a quick, intuitive decision about their car purchase were found to be satisfied with their purchase 60% of the time." Trust your brain's ability to appropriately guide you.

Intuition or gut feelings can also be an expression of your brain's unconscious process which integrates multiple factors. Sometimes we know things without being able to break down or verbalize exactly how or why we think the way we do. We feel pulled to a decision or pushed away from an opportunity, but we cannot clearly define why. Our brains are constantly processing information at a more rapid rate than we can consciously follow. Our brains are integrating things we merely passed over in the day to day life. Our minds are integrating historical knowledge like past experiences or things we have witnessed and projected the likelihood of certain outcomes. Even though we cannot explain these complex processes ourselves, we must trust that our brains have done all of the dirty work. The signals we receive in the form of gut feelings or intuition are the end result of complex processing, millions of synaptic sparks and lots of information integration. Alphas know to trust their brains and their gut feelings. Don't bend to please others. Start setting a trend that you are big and bold. You make decisions for yourself. You care about others. You may compromise or help, but you do not fold on your values and gut feelings just because someone else wants you to be a certain way. If this seems challenging for you, it means you need to start the journey today. Get your head in the right place and stop shoving away your own wisdom and needs. Stand up and read on. You're not alone.

Jack Landry

CHAPTER 3

SPOTTING THE MODERN ALPHA MALE

In a group, look for the guy who takes charge of the conversation effortlessly. He does so unapologetically and will steer the conversation to suit his temperament, mood, and knowledge. Any pregnant pause or any lull in the conversation is seized upon by the alpha male, who takes great pleasure in monopolizing it. He fixes everyone present with his unwavering stare and will never be the first one to break away. He uses his eyes as an effective tool of intimidation and demands attention that way. As far as physicality goes, the alpha male freely touches others appropriately, with or without explicit permission or need. That is done just because he feels so. On the rare occasion when someone else in the group has the floor, if a statement of significant importance is made, everyone turns to the alpha male, as if to respond further keeping his reaction in mind. He leads the pack, figuratively. Everything the alpha male does is deliberate and slow. Clumsy and awkward behavior is for the lower mortals. The top man rises slowly to greet someone or to finish his drink. He will first conclude whatever activity he is engaged in before commencing with another one. He is calm, controlled and deliberate in his actions.

So okay, now you're beginning to get the hang of identifying an alpha male. Please spare a moment for the other guy, the beta male, as well. If there is a dominant personality, submissive behavior is sure to follow. Beta males usually account for almost more than half the male population. Of course, they're all striving to become the next big man or the next alpha male of their group, picking up bits and pieces thrown their way from the big man. Are they happy? Of course not. They are all after the big prize. If you see someone around you who is unduly bossy, who keeps inciting fights and disagreements, tries to prove his masculinity by taking on projects or females or careers that are way above their skill levels, someone who is constantly simmering with unspent anger, thoroughly dissatisfied with life, that's a perfect specimen of a beta male.

What's the moral of this story? What did you understand? Bulging biceps, fierce looking tattoos, physical abuse of women, perhaps a career in boxing or weightlifting are NOT what make an alpha male. It's a tricky combination of nature and nurture. Of hormones and traits and characteristics. Of personality. Not every male is cut out to be an alpha, the leader of the pack. Only a few get to the top.

Genes in the Offing?

Is there a genetic link between alpha behavior and our closest ancestors, the apes? Try and deny it as much as you want, the fact is that such a link exists. Mark Foster, in his alpha male studies, decided to make use of the idea that, in a group, the alpha is always the strongest and biggest animal or person. The *American Journal of Primatology* in 2009 published his findings, which are summarized below.

He studied the shifting of power among three chimpanzees in Tanzania for a period of fourteen years. The largest of the three, Frodo, spent the years literally throwing his weight around the other two, Wilkie and Freud. He was, actually, the largest of the three chimps being studied.

In another study, about ten male chimps were studied for slightly less than a year. Hawks, the experimenter, discovered that not only did the alpha male have all the female attention, the politics of behavior also remained in his charge as long as he was the top chimp in the group.

In yet another study, the male-female relations in respect to the alpha male were observed. The alpha male displayed traits and behavior astonishingly similar to a human alpha male. Just like a ladies' man has his pick of the best of the women and always has them hanging to his arms, the alpha male here was constantly surrounded by the females, waiting for his attention.

Alpha Males in Nature

Alpha males only in the human species? Not a chance. Nature abounds with examples of alpha males in all the species. For instance, take the octopus. He will spend days fending off competition and fighting off other males for his mate. This will go on even when he is actually mating with her. Of course, he will not object to other females entering his territory, disturbing his peace. He might even mate with them. It's only a No Entry board for the males.

The other males do not give up easily, though. They resort to trickery and deception to derive some satisfaction by trying to prevent the alpha male from getting all the females. For example, side blotch lizards, true to their name, spurt bright yellow patches on both sides of their throats. These patches are common to females. Thus disguised, they safely travel within the alpha male's territory. Salamanders take this a step further. Smaller members of the group pretend to court the larger males, frolic around and, when the moment strikes, steal the alpha's sperm and destroy it, to prevent any chance of mating with the females.

Crafty, huh? Wait, there's more. Let's look at some sneaky creatures. There are different kinds of calls in the animal and bird kingdom. Some males take advantage of this fact and give out calls that attract predators. They sneak up close to the alpha male, give a cry and run away into the darkness, presumably to mate with any female who answers the mating call. But in case a predator lurks nearby, the alpha suffers a horrible death and the sneaky betas are free to mate with whoever they wish.

Of course, we also have the good old dung beetles, known for their strong work ethic. Alpha or no alpha, these hardworking beetles build underground dens and hideouts for their fellow beetles and also keep guard. A fighter male always stands guard while mating is taking place inside. They keep darting in and out of the secret places so no predator can snatch them up.

CHAPTER 4

THE PASSIONATE MALE

The most powerful weapon on earth is the human soul on fire. ~Field Marshall Ferdinand Foch

Another characteristic of alpha males is passion, which simply means love for what they're doing. This isn't the kind of love that society, your friends, and your family may necessarily encourage you to have. It's all about what you truly and personally care for and love. It's about your core being.

An example of this would be writing. My mom and most of my friends look down on my choice of trading my corporate (hell) job for freelance writing, which is what I truly love. Truth is, writing has made me come alive in ways that my corporate job never did. In fact, my corporate job killed the real me in many ways! And this was despite a bigger and steadier paycheck!

Now that I feel alive, free, and true to who I really am, I've re-experienced living life with passion again. I no longer drag myself to work because I love what I do for a living! It's not actually work anymore. I get to indulge in two of the best things I love doing for recreation: reading and writing. And that re-ignited passion didn't go unnoticed with my wife. Suffice to say it made me more of an alpha male in her eyes than before I quit my corporate job, which made for a significantly more passionate marriage. Wink, wink!

Personally, I also find that whenever I give talks or seminars on something I'm passionate and knowledgeable about, such as personal finance and investing, people listen to me and follow what my instructions and lead. But when I'm put in situations where I have to talk about or write about something that I'm not passionate about, it shows and people don't seem to take me seriously.

Why is this so? Why is passion so attractive? For one thing, it's because people tend to be drawn toward those who appear to be really sure and certain of the things they themselves are unsure or uncertain about. Passionate people give off this vibe that, more than knowing what they're talking about, they're sure of what they're talking about. Passionate people appear to be so self-assured, transparent, and convinced of the things they say that other people want to be with them.

Living passionately requires a sense of authenticity. A person can't be passionate about something they truly believe in if they're not comfortable under their own skin and if they're always cognizant of having to please others all the time. Once authenticity's a way of living, only then can one live a truly passionate life.

WHAT SEPARATES PASSIONATE MEN FROM THOSE WHO AREN'T?

One thing that's obvious about passionate people is that they live radically different lives from most of those who aren't passionate. Apart from that, here are ten very specific things that passionate people do differently from those who aren't. You can check yourself out in terms of these and see how passionate you are.

-Early Birds: Don't get me wrong; passionate people are entitled to a good night's rest and enough of it. It also doesn't mean that everyone who crows before the rooster does is passionate. What I'm saying is that passionate people tend to start their days early, especially if they're doing something that they're really passionate about. They're just so excited about what they plan to do during the day that they naturally wake up early.

-Consumed by Passion: I'll go out on a limb by saying that really passionate people are obsessed about what they do – in a good and healthy way, of course. Simply put, passionate people's thoughts and actions tend to gravitate toward that which they're passionate about. A pastor or imam who is very passionate about Yahweh or Allah will tend to speak and think – and with passion – around these deities. Human rights activists almost always talk about nothing but the plight of victims of human trafficking whenever they're on TV, radio, or any form of media. And let's face it, remember the last time you got your dream gadget and couldn't stop talking and raving about it for weeks on end to anyone who'd listen?

-More Than the Usual Excitement: It would be weird to assume that passionate people are always jacked up – unless they're on something illegal or caffeinated – acting all excited and jumpy about their passions like the energizer bunny on steroids. No, they're not – they're human! However, passionate people are more excited than the average person, not necessarily in terms of frequency but by the intensity of their expression as well as the lengths they go to for that which they're passionate about. Hard-core runners like Scott Jurek or Dean Karnazes are obviously passionate about running and their excitement is more than the average runner's: they run ultra-marathons (50 kilometers and above) and they run such races often. How many people do you actually know who can run even just a half-marathon at least once a year?

-More than the Usual Disappointment: This is the flipside of being more excited than the average person. Of course, with great passion come great disappointments too! I am passionate about biking and I was extremely disappointed when I realized I couldn't join my friends on a very long ride that I looked forward to for the longest time. My non-biking friends tried to console me but did a very poor job, as they couldn't hide their wonder as to why I'm making such a big deal of not joining a bike ride. Of course they couldn't get it – they don't bike and aren't passionate about it. Well, I guess this heightened disappointment comes with the territory and is a price worth paying occasionally to live a truly alive life.

-Higher Rollers: No, I don't mean they gamble more money than the average person, but passionate people do tend to take on more risk. Why? It's because they believe so much in what they're doing or the cause they're supporting that they believe it's worth the higher-than-usual risk. Again, take for example my passion for biking. I actually ride a fixed-gear bike, which, if you Google it, you'll find to be the riskiest form of urban biking ever. For one, it has no brakes. Anyways, most people scoff at me after finding out that I love urban riding on a fixed gear (fixie for short) bike, thinking I must be out of my mind. But truth is, I simply ride more carefully to minimize the relatively higher risk of riding a bike with no brakes.

-More Devotion: In our lives, we encounter many things that are either worth our time and effort or not. Passionate people tend to focus on what's truly worth their time and effort and, as a result, they tend to devote more time and effort to those things. They're simply good at budgeting their time to what makes the most sense and meaning for them. Good examples are professional bodybuilders. The time, effort, and dedication they have for the sport is nothing short of inhuman. I've never seen a group of people who are as strict in terms of lifestyle as these people are. Why? Because of their passion for the sport.

-Immersed in Their Passion: Many people don't agree with bringing work home but passionate people don't bring their work home, because their work – or whatever it is they're very passionate about – is home. Their lives practically revolve around them. Whether it's family, an advocacy, or a cause, one thing you can clearly see is almost every aspect of their lives either revolves around or reflects aspects of their passions.

-Out of the Abundance of the Heart the Mouth Speaks: Maybe passionate people are already cognizant of the fact that people may be sick and tired of them telling the same things over and over again, albeit in a different way or illustration, but they just can't help themselves. Their hearts are overflowing with what they're passionate about and, as a consequence, they seem to be repetitive in frequently talking about their passions or things related to them.

-All or Nothing: Passionate people are usually extreme– either they go full speed ahead or don't move at all. Their excitement and love for the things they're passionate about can drive them to push themselves to the limit. Most will crash and burn eventually. The good news is that this doesn't happen to all passionate people – only to those who lack wisdom and experience. Those who are seasoned with experience and wisdom are able to manage their passions for sustainable optimal productivity.

-They Got to Wear Shades: Passionate people need to wear shades because they look at the future as so bright and full of potential. They have a very, pardon the pun, sunny outlook on life, which makes them excited and eager to move forward despite risks. This characteristic also gives them the ability to be resilient in the face of setbacks and challenges.

-**They enroll others in their vision:** When you bring passion to the table, you are an instant magician. People who are just inching along in life can be jarred by your self-expression and intrigued. They often see you and ask themselves why they do not have that same zest for life. They live in excuses and hum-drum routines. You shake things up for them. They see new possibilities for themselves when they witness your passion and drive which they want for themselves. You may find they get really interested in you and almost study you. Not only do they want to hear your stories and fantasize about that life for themselves but they want to know your tricks and tools. If you love certain products or attend certain events, they get really interested in doing the same. You enroll them in the things that have worked for you. They think that if they simply follow the things you do, they might live life as passionately as you. This makes you very powerful. You can be powerful to make a contribution to others by inspiring them with your workout routine, diet or meditation practice. They may also see your passion for a charitable or volunteer cause you care about and want to contribute to it as well. You can also profit from their interest if you sell a product or get referral bonuses from certain companies You are the Joneses that people want to mimic.

-**Unapologetic**: Passionate alphas do not wait around for permission from others. They do not wait for someone else to invite them to live life. They find out what they care about and they are not afraid to share it with others. They do not have to test the waters to see if someone else is going to agree with them or like them. They simply live authentically to who they are. They are not afraid to ruffle some feathers or shake up the status quo. Passionate alphas are driven by their vision for their desired world. The way the world is now is irrelevant. They may say things that offend others. Saying something bold that can challenge people's core beliefs can be risky but passionate alphas do not worry themselves about it.

CHAPTER 5

SEE THINGS DIFFERENTLY

The only thing you sometimes have control over is perspective. You don't have control over your situation. But you have a choice about how you view it. ~ Chris Pine, actor

Alpha males act differently from the rest of the human pack because they see things differently. For example, while most other males (omega ones probably), see life as one big people-pleasing party, alpha males see it as THEIR party. While most people believe that being bashful and courteous (only in terms of letting others have their way) is the way to earning people's respect and favor, alpha males believe that such an approach is akin to suicide and that being confident and asserting themselves is the only way to go.

But one thing that holds all this together for the alpha male that most other males don't see is optimism. Alpha males are generally optimistic, particularly about themselves and their situations. They see what's possible instead of what's impossible.

So how can you be optimistic or, if you already are, how can you be even more optimistic? Here are some practical ways for you to do that.

LOOK FOR THE GOOD, NOT THE BAD

One good habit worth cultivating is the habit of seeing the good more than the bad. Now I'm not talking about simply being an alpha-Pollyanna here. No siree! What I'm saying is that alpha males tend to focus more on what's possible instead of impossible, what's workable instead of what isn't, and what good comes out of a situation rather than the bad.

For example, two salesmen make a pitch to a potential client without closing the account. The omega male would dwell and ruminate more on the fact that he didn't close the sale (the bad). He'll probably go to a bar with his friends and talk nothing about how he didn't close the sale and what he probably did wrong – like acting omega!

The alpha male would do it differently. He would, of course, acknowledge the bad, which is the fact that he didn't close the account. But that's as far as he'll go. He'll focus on how he can do things better at the next pitch and the rewards that come with effectively doing it – a closed account! He'll probably not talk about it with his friends later on at their favorite watering hole or if ever he does, he'll probably do so to ask for great ways to do make a better pitch next time.

Having high confidence means that when bad things happen, you do not make it personal about your own deficits. Alphas take responsibility of course since this is the only way to make a change in the future but they do not make it mean something negative about them. A confident person will also see a negative outcome as isolated. You will not see a confident person muttering that this always happens to them or that this is just another example of how they always do something wrong. They see the incident; call a spade a spade and move forward with the expectation that this will not happen again. They are not delusional as they can recognize that they may make a poor choice again in the future, but they do not lose faith in themselves. In psychology, the language used is isolated and external explanations for bad things happening. People who have high self-confidence look at a bad situation or bad outcome and say to themselves "this is just happening this once, and it is not because I am faulty as a person." The opposite is true for people lacking confidence. They will look at a bad outcome and say to themselves "this was bound to happen because it always happens to me and I am fundamentally the problem and will continue to be." The latter type of thinking only perpetuates bad outcomes and consistently induces low self-esteem.

That proactive nature of confident people is consistent across all alphas. They look for solutions. They take action. They don't wait for changes to happen. For them, life does not happen to them. Alphas know they are the source of their lives and their results. This mentality and orientation calls them to take the necessary steps to handle things.

LIST IT DOWN

Listing things at the end of the day, in particular the positive developments, such as closing an account or being able to finish a project milestone, is another good habit to cultivate that will help you be more optimistic and see things much differently than omega males. This is a very good visual reminder of all the good things going your way and it primes your pump for the next day, feeling confident, grateful and positive.

SPEAK IT TO EXPERIENCE IT

The great success guru Anthony Robins once said that our experiences aren't determined by events but by our interpretations of such events. A loved one's death may either be viewed as something to be mourned because of our loss or something to rejoice over because our loved one is at rest after finally being free from pain and suffering. We can, like Thomas Edison, look at failures as discoveries of what not to do to succeed at something, which ultimately brings us much closer to that which will enable us to succeed, or we can look it as a sign from the heavenly bodies that we're not meant to succeed at a given endeavor.

Believe it or not, the ways in which we speak about things shape our experience of such things. It's because our speech is one way of giving suggestions to our subconscious mind, which is what's responsible for how we actually live our lives. We can, literally speaking, speak ourselves into becoming optimistic or pessimistic. The more we consciously speak of positive things about our lives, the more we are able to reprogram our subconscious minds to be more optimistic over time.

LOOK TO YOURSELF

I don't mean this in a narcissistic kind of way. What I mean is that you should focus on what you have instead of what others don't have. One of the biggest reasons for pessimism in the midst of a very good situation is envy of other people. You may be living a very comfortable life where all your needs are being met and more, but if you always look to what the rich and famous athletes like LeBron James and Cristiano Ronaldo have and enjoy, you will feel miserably inadequate and incomplete.

By focusing on what God (or other deities you believe in) or the Universe (if you're more of an atheist) has blessed you with, you'll start to feel more positive about your life. And the funny thing about life is that, the more you're at peace with what you have, the easier it seems for other things to gravitate toward you.

TAKE THE WHEEL

One of the biggest reasons for pessimism is the perception that you are not able to control situations. Some studies have shown that people tend to be more positive about situations that they can exercise a great degree of control over. So what does this mean?

Start living deliberately by beginning to take control over the smaller things in your life, choosing nutritious foods for your diet. Exercise control over this area by ditching sugary drinks for the first week, and sugary food the next. Continue increasing your control over the succeeding weeks by eliminating processed and fried foods until you start eating generally healthy. This way, you take control over one very important aspect of your life: health. Then continue expanding to other areas of your life like fitness and personal productivity. The more areas of your life you're able to control, the more optimistic you'll become in your journey to becoming an alpha male.

Just a word of caution: Be realistic and know that it's impossible to control everything in your life and that some things are just beyond your control. The beautiful thing about taking control of those things in your life that can be controlled is you can also control your responses to those things that you have no control over, which can help you stay positive despite negative developments.

CHAPTER 6

THE SCIENCE OF DOMINANCE

Two distinct studies were conducted on the phenomenon called the alpha male. They yielded some pretty interesting findings. Read on.

Let's call the first subject John. He is 5-foot-10, and has a powerfully fit build. He plays tennis wonderfully well, with great coordination and precision. His strong serve and controlled moves on the court have won him many admirers. Apart from his impressive physicality, he is also extremely competitive, unyielding to pressure, cool and collected under pressure. He has a unique tendency to psychologically dominate and undermine his opponents, often forcing them to make mistakes on the court.

Subject number two is Tim. He is of a slight build, slender and waif-like. He shuffles constantly and gives the feeling of fluidity and movement. Although his serve and returns are consistent, his overall game seems weak and affected. He appears to play for fun, rather than for the competitive spirit. He is laid back and does not mind it if he keeps on losing to his opponents. When faced with stronger and faster opponents, rather than put up a fight, he slows down and backs away, conceding defeat easily. He prefers to form bonds of friendship with the opponents instead of gaining their respect through a tough game.

The participants were asked to write down the characteristics of each of the subjects and rank them in the order of appeal and attractiveness. The researchers then isolated the adjectives and phrases that were coined by the participants. What came up was interesting- while dominance ranked number one in terms of attraction, aggression and domineering personality traits did not feature high in the list.

The second part of the experiment focused on tweaking and fiddling with the description of the first subject. Two descriptions were made: one dominant, the other non-dominant. The group that read the dominant paragraph was told that the subject had participated in a personality test that listed his most extrusive traits as assertive, confident, aggressive, dominant, and demanding. The people reading the non-dominant paragraph were given the phrases laid back, easy going, sensitive, quiet, and shy. This was the experimental group. The other group, the control one, read the description without knowing anything about John's supposed personality test. The women were then asked to pick the adjectives they wanted in a romantic date and those in a long-term romantic partner. The results were astonishing. Only 1 in 50 women ticked "dominant" as a desirable personality trait in a romantic partner. Out of the pool of adjectives, "confident" and "assertive" won hands down. "Demanding" and "aggressive" bit the dust.

Jerry Burger and Mica Cosby did a short follow-up study. They invited 118 female participants to read the exact description of John from the above-mentioned experiment, but they could read only the first three lines of the traits. The study revealed that this time, "dominant" and "aggressive" John was preferred over "shy" and "quiet" John.

Perception matters more than reality. This is true through and through when putting yourself out there with other people. This is a great argument for the "fake it until you make" perspective. You do not need to feel like you have totally sorted out your life before you feel confident. You simply act confident. You may find new ways of seeing the challenges you have, too. If you see yourself as smart, capable and confident while acting in accordance with that, people start to see you differently. When people start to see you differently, they naturally treat you differently. Guess what that means? You get new results. Just by playing the part of a confident alpha, you start getting the results of a confident alpha. Remember, being an alpha really has little to do with your innate makeup. It has way more to do with how you present yourself. If you cut an alpha open, you may see very little differences than if you cut a beta open. Stop waiting around for the perfect moment. No matter how much you work out or hone your public speaking, you may never feel totally ready to be a fool-proof alpha. So skip all of the hassles and live like an alpha now.

This is the difference between doing and being. "Doing" the life of an alpha may suggest you would go to the gym or have a certain corporate job. You might conjure images of being surrounded by beautiful women or having a healthy bank account. You might imagine an alpha telling jokes that draw a crowd at a cocktail party. From this perspective, if you do not have all of those skills and competencies yet, you may be intimidated by the thought of being an alpha. You may get stuck like a deer in headlights at the mental "to do" list that you instantly generate with those ideas. However, if you are thinking about "being" an alpha, it is totally different. You realize you have the tools at your fingertips today. Not tomorrow or in 3 years when you do X, Y or Z. "Being" an alpha involves only the decision to be so and the practice of following your gut as you move forward. When you "be" something, you act from a place that you are a certain way and the world adjusts in alignment with it. Some people struggle with this concept. They throw the idea away before it is even tested. Try it. Decide one evening that you will be an alpha in a new crowd. Maybe you are traveling for work to a new city or at a conference. Even if you find a new watering hole in your own area, this can work. Go into a crowd that does not yet know you (and whatever your past self is) and "be" an alpha. Take a moment to set yourself up ahead of time. This could be a quick visualization in your car or some power posing (that's right, puffed chest and all) in front of the mirror. Conjure up all of the images and traits of the alpha you are aspiring to be. Decide at that moment that for the next few hours you will simply embody the alpha. Do not break character. Live it fully. Any hiccups that happen do not matter. Remember, an alpha doesn't let others or the world give them signs that something is wrong with them. They simply let things roll off their backs and get back to being the life of the party. Try this experiment and you will not be sorry. Fake it until you make it.

CHAPTER 7

RESILIENCY

"Resiliency is all about being able to overcome the unexpected. Sustainability is about survival. The goal of resilience is to thrive." ~ Jamais Cascio

Alpha males don't back down from challenges and adversity. Being comfortable with being themselves, knowing their strengths and capabilities and with a positive outlook that believes in what is possible, alpha males are able to persist until they get what they want, be it a woman, a position, or a goal they set for themselves.

It's resiliency that allows alpha males to get any woman they fancy after her initial attempts to fend him off. This resiliency sends the message that the man is a leader, is the top dog, is alpha, and is in control of the situation. Women also find this sexy.

It's resiliency that allows alpha males to reach the top of the corporate ladder despite the dog-eat-dog competition and many disappointing events on the way there. If the alpha male isn't resilient, he won't get to the top and be the leader. In which case, he won't even be alpha.

Knowing the importance of resiliency in being an alpha male, here are practical ways to be resilient or to become even more resilient.

GOALS

If you don't know why you're doing what you're currently doing, you will easily fold at the first instance of challenges and failures. Why? It is human nature to be motivated only by two things: seeking pleasure and avoiding pain. If you're fully aware of the greater pleasure you're seeking or the greater pain you're trying to avoid, you can persist even in the midst of challenges.

Take, for example, a working student who grew up in poverty. If he's sick and tired of living in poverty, he'll definitely want to move up from his current social class to either avoid the discomforts of his current economic status or to experience so much pleasure associated with being financially successful. To that extent, he'll find the discomforts of getting very little sleep every day and scrimping on most other things he'd want to spend on for the next couple of years as he juggles finishing his collegiate studies and working at Burger King in order to have a shot at living his dream. For most people, who have no dreams or goals such as his, they'd quit after the very first day. But a person with such dreams will persist until he gets hold of those dreams.

Use the SMARTER methodology that coaches the world overuse with their clients. SMARTER is specific, measurable, achievable, realistic, time-bound, evaluate and redo or reflect. This approach can be very effective for almost any type of goal. So start with a vision for yourself and then fit it into this model. You may want to adjust some things when you start asking yourself if the original timeline you had in mind is realistic for example. The evaluate part refers to giving yourself checkpoints to see how you are progressing. The redo or reflect part means that you can leave space to see if you want to shift the goal a bit. Do you need a bit more time? Do you have another path toward your end result that has arisen since you made the plan? Smart people make SMARTER goals. They don't just hope something comes true. They make it happen.

KNOW YOURSELF

Resiliency also depends on how capable you know yourself to be. To this extent, it is very important to have an honest and accurate idea of your strengths and weaknesses. If for example, you know you're good at writing instead of math, it'll be more realistic to persist in self-publishing rather than becoming a physicist. Doing otherwise will not lead to success.

Successful people find ways to express their strengths each day. Their work and volunteering often map directly onto their strengths. Everybody wins when you are shining your brightest. If your strengths are not obvious to you, then start by thinking about a peak experience. Think about a time when you felt really proud of your accomplishments.

Maybe it was a time when other people were really impressed by you too. Chances are, if you were excelling then, you were using your strengths. Dissect that experience for a minute. What were you doing? What skills were you using? The attributes are critical to your self-knowledge.

Resiliency isn't blind positivity. It also requires wisdom, in particular concerning what you can and you can't realistically achieve. To this extent, knowing yourself well is key. It's best to also get the input of some of your most trusted and objective friends, coworkers, classmates, or business partners to be able to objectively evaluate your strengths and weaknesses. Some people may shy away from giving us direct feedback, especially on the weakness side. Make sure to ask in a way where you get the information you need. You might try "what kinds of things could I work on to be a stronger employee (or leader, or husband, or father or friend)?" You could also try "what are things I do that really make a difference? Make a contribution?" These questions occur to people in a more developmental way, so they are not afraid to share in order to help you.

RELATIONSHIPS

Surrounding yourself with people who can support, encourage and advise you wisely is very important in becoming a resilient person. Let's face it, there are times when you'll probably doubt yourself or wouldn't know what to do to overcome certain challenges or sticking points. Having a dependable support team can help you get over certain humps that you may not be able to do so alone.

I have a friend who even put together a life advisory board. He realized that (partly because he was so good at so many things and so in demand) he was filling his life up a little too full. He hated saying "no" to great opportunities, but he knew something needed to give. That's when he invited a few trusted people in his life to help him with decisions. Whenever a new book deal, contract or offer would come up, he would send it to this group, and they would vote on whether he would take it on or not. He said it was really helpful to get a rational decision made by people he trusted. Things really worked out. Now obviously, this is formalized and a little uncommon. However, most of us engage our closest people in less formal ways but to the same end. We'll share over a beer or a BBQ the kinds of things happening in our lives and value the feedback or reaction we get. That is why it is critical to be thoughtful about people we spend time with. There really is something to the idea that people are the average of the five people they spend the most time with. They are an average weight of those they spend their weekends with, they have a similar attitude to those they lunch with at work, and they have a relatively similar bank statement to those they spend their evenings with. The conversations that happen with those we spend time with completely shape how we see the world.

Be choosy. Alphas do not shy away from driving the agenda or calling out things that just bring them down but at the same time, it is helpful to be with people who see things how you see them. Be careful to choose your support team well and ensure that they're qualified. It's good to diversify. You may want to include encouraging people, challenging people, spiritual people, and business-savvy people to help you hurdle many different challenges.

LOVE CHANGE

The ability to adapt to any situation is another important characteristic of a resilient person. Resilient people are able to use crises and other challenging life situations as springboards for achieving their goals faster or for launching into a new and better direction than originally planned. Most people are significantly affected by sudden changes in life situations and are discouraged from moving on, but resilient ones look at such changes as possible allies.

OPTIMISTIC

Optimism is an important part of resiliency because without it, hope is lost. As mentioned earlier, it may not come naturally for you but by cultivating certain habits, you can become a naturally optimistic alpha male.

If you don't think of optimism as a habit, it may be because you either already do the habit, or you don't see it as something you can develop within you. Optimism is an expressed skill. Maybe this statement is blowing your mind or drawing out the inner cynic. Researchers in the new field of positive psychology have started defining traits of optimism (hopeful orientation to the future, positive explanatory style and so on). They have done experiments where pessimistic people must be on a schedule to engage in optimistic behaviors. They are given clues like a message on their cell phone to be optimistic. The results are staggering. They start acting optimistic, and soon enough it becomes a trend for them. A habit if you will. They have taken off their dark lenses and donned new perhaps more rose-colored ones. Again, realism still has a place. Being hopeful doesn't take the place of doing what needs to be done. You must watch for signs of needing to change direction or do more to get to that desired future. The baseline is always that you see that future as being possible. That is optimism plain and simple. Rob yourself of that and good luck getting what you want down the line. If you don't see it as possible, your actions will never line up to make it so.

LOVE YOURSELF

No, we're not promoting selfishness or self-centeredness here. We're talking about loving yourself just enough to be able to take good care of it. Often, resilient people can be too absorbed in powering through a situation that they neglect their own needs, such as adequate sleep, physical fitness, and proper nutrition, which eventually aggravate their situation.

To be a resilient person, don't hesitate to take care of yourself by getting enough sleep, eating right, exercising, and indulging yourself once in a while in things that you love. Doing so helps give you the power you need to thrive.

Loving yourself also means saying "no." You honor yourself, what you need and what matters to you by living in alignment with your priorities. This may mean you need to piss a few people off. At the same time, they begin to mentally register that you have boundaries. There is nothing fundamentally wrong with saying "no." It just means that you are not obliging the person making the request of you at that time on that particular topic. Do not let your tendency to please people get in the way of what you need. Care about yourself, your mind and your body. Let those things factor into your decision making. Neglect them for any length of time and watch the results. You will start to decline either in energy or creativity. You may even get really sick. Our bodies have a miraculous way of slowing us down. It can be getting the flu for a week, or it can be much more serious. Watch for signs early on and be proactive. You cannot both truly love yourself and also be bad to yourself at the same time. Those two notions cannot co-exist. Do what you know to do. A little self-care goes a long way to true longevity and thriving. When you're at the top of your game, resiliency is just part of the package.

PATIENCE

Lastly, be patient with yourself. There are times that too much resiliency can also be harmful, in the sense that you may overwork yourself just to be able to succeed faster. Just remember, a victory worth experiencing is one that's worth waiting for.

That doesn't mean being lax or negligent. No, God forbid. No. What this means is that, after doing the best that you can, allow those efforts to naturally bear their fruit.

CHAPTER 8

CHARACTERISTICS OF THE ALPHA MALE

Social dominance is associated with several different personal characteristics, both physical and non-physical. They're also divided into those that can be changed or modified and those that can't be. Let's start with physical traits that make most alpha males that can't be changed much, or are fixed for life.

So, what makes an alpha male alpha? Does he have some extra traits or special qualities, which make him so desirable to the opposite sex? Let's find out.

Physical Characteristics

1. Height: Let's face it – tall people enjoy significantly more social benefits than those who aren't. For one, taller guys are less sensitive to other men's dominance cues such as masculinity and hence aren't intimidated easily or at all. They also tend to be less jealous of equally dominant – social and physical – men compared to shorter ones. Tall men are also looked at as dominating over shorter ones.

Yes, these are just physical characteristics and not all short men have an inferiority complex but, generally speaking, taller men tend to be more confident and dominant and, as a result, they enjoy more perks. For example, taller men generally have more access to leadership roles, enjoy higher beginning pay, and greater income overall. This is not necessarily because they're tall but because of the social proof or perception that they're stronger or more dominant.

Socially speaking, particularly in the dating scene, height is also a highly valued commodity. Let's face it, you never hear of women who say they want to be with a dude who's short, dark, and handsome, right? Apart from the impression that taller dudes have longer and bigger dangles, height is perceived as being sexy and dominant, characteristics many women look for in a potential mate these days.

Despite height being a physical characteristic of social dominance in many cases, it doesn't mean it's the case all the time. While it's true that being tall makes it easier for a man to be socially dominant, it's not a sure thing. In fact, not all tall men are socially dominant. Not all are alpha.

Being tall is definitely an advantage, with a range of proven social benefits. Taller men are perceived as more successful in their endeavors, as possessing more masculinity, as being dominant, as able to take charge, and as socially superior. Studies have proven that taller men enjoy increased starting salaries and more responsible positions at their workplaces. One study demonstrated that almost all the top shots in companies, the CEOs, the CFOs, the MDs, the managers were much taller than the average employee who mans the visitors' desk or sits in a cubicle or operates the company telephone.

Of course, height is also a very valuable trait in the dating and mating market. Ask any woman what she wants in a man and the most likely attribute to come out of her mouth first will be "tall." Experiments and studies have shown that not only do women prefer taller men in controlled lab conditions, they do so in real life, as well. Take any dating scenario: real life, online, through advertisements, speed dating. The taller men are snapped up first. This is also because height is directly correlated with virility and masculinity. Therefore, a shorter man, no matter how winning his personality may be, will take a back seat to the taller man.

2. Voice: Have you ever heard Barry White's voice? Oh, man, it makes even the alpha males go soft. So deep and sexy! Or how about James Earl Jones? Wouldn't that voice make you stand up and just follow orders? So manly...so dominant!

Studies have shown that a man's voice does a better job of communicating dominance than spoken words. If I threaten you by saying, "I'm gonna beat you to a bloody pulp if you don't obey!" with a tweety bird voice, you're not gonna take me seriously, right? Right! Now if I told you, "I'd appreciate if you stay out of my territory, ya' hear?" in with the voice of Vin Diesel or Michael Jai White, I think it would strike more fear in your heart, right? Right again!

Especially a for men who's not yet been seen, a big voice communicates that he may be the size of Shaquille O'Neal and as such, you may want to avoid running into him especially when he already told you in his big, badass voice that "If you don't pray often, the best time to start doing so is now." Lastly, men with low and big voices tend to be perceived as – I don't know why – older, braver and wiser.

Lastly, men who sound like Barry White, James Earl Jones, Vin Diesel, or Michael Jai White tend to have more fun in the sack, if you know what I mean. Why? Women simply find low, big voices manlier and consequently sexier.

A deep bass voice signals more testosterone, more masculinity and more maturity, drawing women toward it like moths to a flame. The tone of the voice speaks volumes about the man. The deeper the voice, the more manly and aggressive the personality and the more ability to potentially fight and protect his loved ones. Men with deeper voices are generally perceived to be taller, more successful, dominant, and mature. A high-pitched voice has always been associated with the female species. Going back in evolutionary history, the female needed to be able to shout and warn others if danger lurked in the corner. She needed different voice modulations to match the moods and emotions of others around her. But the male remained strong and silent, speaking only when necessary. Thus, a deeper baritone signifies strength, maturity, wisdom, a sense of responsibility and control. Now, which woman can resist these qualities in a man? Studies have also revealed that men with such euphonious voices displayed higher mating successes and fathered more children. No wonder women find deep voices alluring and hard to resist.

3. Face: One's facial features can also factor into his ability to dominate socially, especially with first impressions. A handsome face isn't necessarily one that's socially dominating; it depends on what kind of handsome. There are ruggedly handsome men and there are boyishly handsome men and there are handsomely cute men who look as if they'll make great pets or home decors, i.e., they're so adorable. When it comes to social dominance, you can scrap the boy-next-door and cutesy patootsy kinds of handsome because they don't evoke dominance – they evoke softness. Ruggedly handsome looks take the cake because rugged conveys the impression of tough, strong,

and sturdy. Some women even find scars to be sexy, say those of Tom Hardy's, which is a sign that he's gone through something awful and was strong enough to live and tell the tale.

A rugged face, with many planes and angles, is believed to trigger deep-seated emotional responses in women. Such men are highly prized, with women believing that a scruffy and rugged visage holds great promise genetically. It promotes masculinity like nothing else. Soft, smooth, rounded faces or heart shaped faces are correlated with femininity. A strong masculine face with planes immediately attracts the opposite sex. If there are any scars or battle lines on the face, the better. It means that the man has fought hard battles and has not shied away from displaying his battle scars.

This particular feature has received considerable interest from researchers. An actual accurate measurement tool has been developed by scientists to measure and assess the facial attributes in male faces: the ratio of the width of the face (f) to the upper limit of the height of the face (WHR). Men who had higher ratios also had proportionally higher levels of testosterone. A wide, rugged face with day-old stubble is not only incredibly sexy to look at; it denotes a sense of carefree well-being, importance, success, and power. Such men are perceived as formidable opponents, and they also make ferocious fighters, thus accentuating their appeal with the opposite sex.

4. Size: If you look around at nature and even otherwise, you almost never find puny, short fellows making their mark, unless spectacularly gifted. Size does matter, and the men who are bigger in size see greater gains in business, relationships, and fights. A bigger size directly correlates to dominance and aggression and success. A display of size is usually made by standing with feet wide apart, hands on the hips and adopting an intimidating stance.

5. Eye contact: An unwavering eye contact makes the person look dominant and in charge of the situation. Unblinking eyes can also sometimes unnerve other people, who might look away or down at the floor. People who do that are perceived to be sneaky, hiding something, maybe even lying. An open, direct stare puts all doubts to rest.

6. Physically fit: Look at any successful man. Open the magazines or newspapers, or switch your TV on. What do you see? Are any of the top biz men fat? With ungainly

paunches? No. All of them are at the top of their game. Being physically fit is a powerful alpha attribute. A trim and athletic body conveys to people that the male in question is serious about keeping himself in top physical condition. It is also a throwback to the early days, when man could not afford to be lazy and unfit. Any misstep and he could lose his life in a duel. Fitness is therefore an undeniable characteristic.

7. Body language and personality: Have you seen a successful man slouch and walk slowly? Or perhaps wear wrinkled clothes? Or maybe clasp and unclasp his hands during a meeting, with eyes darting to and fro? Yeah, me neither. Carefully study the traits and body language of people who are perceived to be flourishing and thriving in their fields. Look at them. They emanate confidence and radiance. They are always groomed properly, have a spring in their step, look other people in the eye, their handshake is firm; they seem to exude an inner glow of surety and conviction. People feel safe around them and trust them implicitly. Weaker people look up to them to make decisions and come up with ideas. A strong, positive body language has always been the hallmark of an alpha male.

Gestures and Other Characteristics

- Touching: In a group, the person doing all the touching may either be a certified pervert or an alpha. The difference lies in the intensity of the touch and who is doing the touching. A non-emotional touch, like a pat on the head or the back or the shoulders, is a sign of dominance and superiority. Betas and omegas usually do not initiate any physical contact first. It is always the alphas who do so. They touch other people freely, without hesitation, and with or without explicit permission.

- Confidence: This is the hallmark of an alpha male. A weak person with low self-esteem and image issues can never hope to lead the pack or the group. People always turn to the leader, the man with self-control, someone who has immense confidence in himself and his abilities.

- Mentally tough: An alpha male is also perceived as possessing mental toughness, a very desirable quality if he has to outwit and outperform his competitors to stay at the top of his game. His decisions are always spot on; he never wavers from his stand and has the courage to go against the flow.

- Competitive: Men who compete actively are seen as more desirable and successful than those who play the game just for the heck of it or for the fun of it. A competition is more serious. There will be a winner and a loser and alphas rarely, if ever, lose to anyone. A strong competitive streak is a supreme alpha trait.

- Calm under pressure: Ever seen a CEO or a president yelling at his subordinates or breaking things in view or mouthing obscenities in case of a failure? No, right? The man at the top always keeps a cool and calm head under pressure and deals with the situation head on. Instead of venting his anger and frustration in silly and destructive activities, he takes a controlled approach and looks for solutions to the problems instead of creating more with his behavior. Therefore, a cool presence and controlled behavior and approach are seen as the traits of the top men, the alphas, and wrecking behavior is more often attributed to the lower rungs in the hierarchy.

- No external validation: Some people need constant reassurance from their peers, family, and bosses that they are doing something right. Not the alpha male. He is secure, has no doubts about his abilities, and certainly does not need an outside perspective and opinion in order to feel good about himself. He already knows he is at the top of the ladder and his internal motivation is so great that no external forces are required to substantiate his existence.

- Growth potential: A successful alpha believes in growth. Be it personal or professional, he knows that the only way ahead is forward and upward. No blame games for him, either. He owns up to his mistakes and strives to learn from them. He never makes the same mistake twice. He also believes in giving people second chances.

- A problem solver: Instead of sitting around, bemoaning the lack of resources or good people to work with or the work atmosphere, the alpha takes charge of the situation. He goes all out to make sure the hurdles in his path are crossed amicably.

- Fearless: An alpha is never the one to shy away from problems or mistakes. He takes it all head on. Problems always come with a solution and every mistake is a learning step for him. Repenting over the loss of something is not in his dictionary. He owns up, rectifies the error, and moves on.

- Passionate and ambitious- Alpha males are always driven. They take up projects and issues with a fervor and passion unmatched by others and they deliver. No empty promises. They aim high, strive to reach their goals with the resources available to them, and make good on their promises. Everything they do bears the stamp of their passion and love for the project at hand.

- High moral ground- You will never find an alpha straying from his principles and values. He has a certain set of principles that he adheres to religiously and no amount of external coercion can lead him astray from his path.

Some of the qualities mentioned here, such as leadership, good grooming, and being calm under pressure are vital to an alpha male. They are discussed in further detail in the next chapters.

CHAPTER 9

COMPOSED UNDER PRESSURE

Every negative – pressure, challenges – is all an opportunity for me to rise. ~ Kobe Bryant

An alpha male is one who is graceful under fire, composed under pressure. Why? Being confident about themselves and their situations, they know that they can handle whatever challenge is in front of them – be it having to go up to a hot woman in the bar and come home with her or making a successful pitch to a client who's known to devour lesser mortals. With women and business, alpha males don't buckle under pressure; they thrive in it and succeed.

So how can you cultivate the characteristic of being composed while under pressure? Here are practical ways to do so.

APPRECIATE

One of the reasons why people buckle under pressure is that they don't appreciate enough what they already have and therefore they fear losing out on those things they hope to gain by overcoming certain challenges. This thinking makes for desperation, believing that the only way to have something to appreciate is by overcoming challenges alone. When desperate, people tend to be more nervous, anxious, and stressed, which makes for buckling under pressure much more likely.

When you cultivate the habit of appreciating what you have, you'll tend to think of the rewards associated with overcoming challenges as merely bonuses; that there's nothing to lose, really. With such an attitude, you won't feel desperate, which you just read to be a precursor to nervousness, anxiety, and stress – ingredients for increasing your risk of buckling down under pressure.

Being grateful isn't just beneficial psychologically, it's physiological too. It helps bring down levels of cortisol, a stress hormone. Less cortisol, less stress, and less chance of buckling under pressure.

FOCUS

One of the worst things you can do in a pressure-packed situation is to ask about the myriad ways that things can go wrong. It's like pouring gasoline over a bonfire, you know. By asking about many different ways things can go wrong if you don't handle the pressure situation right, you're just adding more things to worry about and you overload your mind.

Simply focus on doing what needs to be done so that you don't take on unnecessary stress. By focusing, you can stay relatively calm and clear-headed enough to successfully address a pressure-packed situation.

By doing this, you also become a good person to work with in these types of situations. People know you as a rock. They see that you do not get wrapped up in the problems or the things that might go wrong. They see your orientation is toward doing what is needed and staying the course.

Successful people rarely fly off the handle. They are stable-minded. If things go wrong, they handle it by examining what is needed. They do not add drama. They focus on actions and resolve. This kind of composure instills confidence in others that your leadership can be trusted. They see that the world works the way you say it works. Things turn out the way you say. Why? Because they see you are the source of things in the same way, you see yourself. You are not reacting fervently to things coming at you. You are crafting things yourself. This is why you keep your composure – because you see that you have a say in how things turn out.

POSITIVE THINKING

Thinking positive things help give your mind intermittent relief from stress and anxiety. Without such relief, your mind will easily tire out from thinking (and worrying?) and that will keep you from staying calm and composed during pressure-packed situations.

Any positive thought can go a long way to help you out. However, it's best to look back on those that really gave you some of the greatest joy or look forward to some great reward associated with overcoming the situation. The most important thing is to give your mind a break and a boost so that you can stay calm and composed during your challenging situation.

Looking back on the positive can reaffirm your capability to move through something hard. If you have been able to do it before, you can trust in your ability to pull it off again. That type of thinking can help give you the confidence you need to take the next step and keep your cool. Thinking positively about your team and resources is also helpful. When you are grateful for the energy and skills of those around you, you set up a situation where they want to deliver. When they know you believe in them and have expectations of them, the natural human response is to fall in line with that. Positivity gives you a certain orientation to your situation which, in turn, gives you your next action steps. We only interact with the world the way we see it. When we see it as something that will deliver good things, we tend to get those results.

DETACH

Knowing the value of intermittent relief for our minds during stressful situations, regularly detaching from situations for much-needed breathers can be very beneficial in terms of being calm and composed under pressure. Stress is similar to temptations in that the best approach is to avoid or minimize exposures to them. By regularly detaching from your stressors or challenging situations, you can help give your mind and body much-needed rest and a boost.

A change of pace or activity can be helpful. When we are involved in intellectual pursuits, we sometimes find ourselves in situations where our minds grow tired. We work and work at something yet we become less effective at getting the desired results. This is a good sign that you need a break. A break can be playing a computer game or reading something you enjoy. It could be having a chat with someone or listening to music. Often, a great break for our minds is to do something physical. When we get our attention on our bodies, we take a much-needed intellectual break. We stop trying to figure something out by staring right at it. We could run, walk, dance, do push-ups or shoot some hoops. The funny thing about the change of scenery is that we often find solutions to our problems when we get our heads in a different place. Our subconscious minds are always working even when our conscious minds are doing something new. After a little mental break, we return to something and find we are much more creative. The answer may become obvious. So stop working hard when you just aren't getting anywhere. Take a break, switch gears and then go back to it refreshed. If you value keeping a lid on your frustration or anger, you will give yourself breaks before you start to steam.

CAFFEINE

If you want to be able to significantly reduce nervousness and anxiety under pressure-packed situations, ditch the caffeine. Why? Caffeine releases adrenaline, which is our bodies' flight-or-fight response trigger. This response system, which is responsible for preserving the human race during more dangerous times, tends to override rational thinking in order to act quickly and survive.

When adrenaline runs through our blood, our minds and bodies tend to be in a super-aroused stress state, which can drown out logical behavior. If you can't wean yourself from caffeine completely, go for significantly cutting down on your regular consumption and ditching it whenever you're faced with a pressure-packed situation. Switching to black tea can be a good transition away from coffee.

Sometimes we can get into a bad habit of using caffeine to compensate for not taking care of ourselves. So instead of watching our diets to make sure we are fueling ourselves with energizing foods, we will just eat badly and then use caffeine to give us energy. We might stay up late watching shows or drinking and then feel sluggish the next day. What do we do? We have some espresso and try to compensate. This pattern is hard on our bodies and not particularly sustainable. If we are using caffeine in this way, we can behave strangely. Because we are actually tired but trying to cover it up with a little liquid energy, we sometimes have brain blips. This happens when our bodies are energized and ready to go (adrenaline) but our minds are a little slow. We have the tendency to want to do things and jump into conversations, but our minds are not processing very fast. It is far better to take care of yourself and use caffeine moderately. You will be able to engage appropriately and act as needed when challenges arise.

SLEEP

One of the biggest contributors to any person's sense of stress, anxiety, and nervousness is lack of sleep. Sleep is the mind's window of opportunity to rest and recharge, so it only makes sense that chronic lack of sleep leads to heightened stress, anxiety, and nervousness, all of which affect one's ability to handle pressure-packed situations. When we sleep, our brains integrate the new knowledge of the day and make the necessary neural connections, so we retain new information. When we deny our brains the time to do this, it can lead to forgetfulness and confusion. It's like we packed our trunk for vacation but we never closed the door. Suddenly all of the good stuff we put in there falls out. It is a waste of your time, and it dishonors the actions you took during your waking hours.

Do yourself a favor and get enough sleep. What's enough? Experts agree that it's anywhere between 6 to 8 hours depending on individual situations and lifestyles. Try sleeping in without an alarm for the next few days and note how you feel during those days. It'll give you a good idea of what's optimal for you. Great sleep hygiene cannot be emphasized enough. Having a routine before sleeping helps cue your body that it is time to start winding down. If you use the same toothpaste, sleep on the same side of the bed, read before sleep and so on, you gear your body up to enter REM sleep faster. REM sleep stands for rapid eye movement. This is the stage of sleep that causes you to feel most rested. It is a stage where you dream, and your body takes care of itself. Avoiding caffeine in the afternoon and evening help give way to better sleep and less restlessness. Leaving a gap between your last meal and sleeping also allows for restful sleep because digestion is already completed. When you are well-rested, your mind is much sharper to troubleshoot problems and find solutions. Be kind to yourself – unwind.

PERSPECTIVE

In most cases, anxiety, stress, and nervousness result from the way we see things. While it's true that deadlines that are nowhere near realistic, bosses that seem to have been born and raised in another universe, and traffic that seems to get worse by the day are why we are so stressed and anxious, truth is that it's how we respond to them that really affect us.

If our nervousness and anxiety over something is mostly due to the way we think about it, then reframing our perspective will help go a long way toward helping to stay calm and composed in pressure-packed situations. This discipline may take time to develop, especially if you've been used to it. Take heart, you can change that habit and be able to reframe your perspective as naturally as breathing with enough time and practice.

Reframing means that you look at something and ask yourself what your belief about that thing is. Here's a hint — the belief is often about ourselves. So if we have a big deadline looming, we might think "I'm not smart enough to do that" or "they might not like what I come up with." Ideas like this can add a lot of unnecessary stress to something and dampen our creative process. Often these ideas sit there in our minds unexamined. They absolutely shape what we do and how we feel about things, yet we often don't recognize that they are there. We certainly don't recognize the dire impact they have on our mental wellness or our ability to take something on. If we did recognize this, we would definitely resolve it. So when reframing, identify what the belief is. Then fill out the story of why we believe that's true. I'm talking just a minute of reflection, nothing too big. It could be that you had a hard time delivering on something once before or that you know your boss can be critical. Next, look at the truths in it such as the limitations that you legitimately have. Like if you are asked to use a computer program to do something but you are not very skilled with it yet. Or maybe you acknowledge you have procrastinated so long that it will be difficult to complete it on time. These are great things to recognize. Next, look at the opposite side of the coin. Identify how that belief you have is kind of bull. Think of the times you have disproven it for example. Then look back at the belief and see if it still rings true. Likely it will not. So then choose a new belief. In the process, because you were able to hone in on some genuine challenges, you have just named the things you need. If you have procrastinated, that points toward a solution that is getting other people involved and delegating so you can still make your deadline or otherwise ask for an extension. By reframing, you drop the heavy thinking and start being solution-focused.

BREATHE

One of the quickest ways to be combat nervousness, stress and anxiety under pressure-packed situations is to breathe properly. It has a physiological effect, slowing down your racing heartbeat and running mind. You've heard people talk about the mind-body connection. So sometimes you've probably used the concept of "mind over matter" to do something like persevere through something challenging, lift something big or bite your tongue when you were bursting inside and wanting to smack someone. You used your mind and self-talk to keep your body calm. It might help to think now about the body-mind connection. This is a little twist. It remembers that this connection can work to our advantage to calm our mind too. We simply put our body into a state of calm, and our mind follows. This feedback loop between mind and body is constantly running.

Here's how to do it. Whenever you're feeling anxious, nervous, or stressed, get away to a secluded spot. Sit down and take a deep belly breath[1] in 3 to 4 seconds, hold it for 2 seconds before exhaling all the air out in 3 to 4 seconds.

---

[1] Expand your belly as you breathe and keep your chest and shoulders steady.

Repeat five times and notice how much less anxious, stressed, and nervous you are. It really takes just a minute and can transform your whole mental and bodily experience. You can physically reduce your blood pressure and heart rate just through this simple practice. Or, you could watch things escalate and hope you don't boil over. Be proactive and when the going gets tough, take a beat to breathe and then return with a calm mind and body.

CHAPTER 10

A LEADER

A leader is one who knows the way, goes the way and shows the way. ~John C. Maxwell

Who is a leader? Well, a leader is a person who is able to influence a group of people to achieve goals and objectives. In other words, a leader is a person that people follow.

When it comes to modern leadership, it is believed leaders aren't necessarily born – they're developed or raised. Some people, however, seem to be so comfortable and natural as leaders that it seems leadership is a genetic trait or inborn.

Alpha males are leaders. They may not lead everyone they know but they do take the lead in most, if not all, of their social circles. Many of them are natural leaders, not necessarily born, but natural in the sense that, over time, they may have accidentally developed it through their experiences and situations.

How about you? Are you a natural leader? If you want to find out, simply answer these questions:

-Do you really, really want something?

-Is it natural for you to go after that which you want?

-Can you enlist other people to help you go after what you want?

If you answered yes to the third question, chances are that you're a natural leader. If you're not, there's good news and bad news. The bad news is that you may have a harder time achieving most of your goals and dreams. It's because most things worth achieving require the help of others.

The good news is that leadership is a skill and, as such, it can be developed. With enough time, resilience, and smarts, you can develop leadership skills, much as you can learn how to bike or cook. The amount of time it may take for you to do it will vary greatly but, believe me, it's worth it.

POWER AND INFLUENCE

As mentioned earlier, alpha males are leaders and leadership is about the ability to make people follow you. There are two ways of doing this: power and influence. Power is the ability to impose one's will on other people and to make things happen by compelling subordinates to obey instructions or commands. A person can use power wisely or unwisely. Power is such a tricky thing that it needs to be used sparingly and only when needed, as it can lead to potential abuses by the leader or resentments in the subordinates. Influence, on the other hand, is the ability to make people want to follow you out of their own free will.

POWER

Power has three sources: legitimate power, reward power, and coercive power.

Legitimate power comes from a person's status or position in a group or organization. Simply put, legitimate power is one that can't be questioned, such as legal authority. Take a cop, for example. If you break the law, a cop has the legal authority to arrest you regardless of how you plead or appeal to your daddy's position in the government. Your daddy can't – legally at least – compel the cop to drop the charges against you even if he's the president of the United States! That's legitimate power right there!

Alpha males rarely use legitimate power. Alpha males are primarily social leaders and relationships hardly ever develop or become strong through authoritarian rule. Just look at communist or authoritarian regimes – practically all of them have already died out. Only a handful remains but they are also on the brink of collapse because the members of the group they lead are becoming increasingly dissatisfied with it.

Reward power is a leader's ability to reward members of the group for obedience or jobs well done. In business, these include promotions, salary increases, awards, or other career incentives. Social rewards include social proof or affirmation, prestige, fame, and honor, among others. Alpha males, to some extent, exercise reward power, but not deliberately. It's merely a result of who they are. Alpha males are some of the most popular and most sought-after people, making their acceptance and approval very great reward. Many people seek acceptance and approval and, as such, many of them tend to follow alpha males. Even without trying, the alpha male exercises reward power.

Lastly, coercive power is the exact opposite of rewarding. Here, a leader uses threats and punishments to make members of a group follow him. An example of this would be a dad threatening he'll throw his rebellious son out of the house to live on the streets if he doesn't change his behavior. Here we start to see a distinction between power and force. When people have power, they do not need to use force. They do not need to strong arm people into following them or listening to their ideas. Instead, they are charismatic and inspirational. They can elicit support and action from others without making others do things. This coercive power or force does not look good on anyone. It looks like you are weak just trying to push something through. When you are powerful, you can move mountains with your words and have natural influence with people. That is a much better look on anyone.

An alpha male seldom resorts to coercive power, if ever. For one, coercive power is an option of last resort, when position or rewards aren't enough to make an insolent member toe his leadership line. As such, it reeks of desperation and alpha males aren't desperate. They naturally make people want to follow them.

INFLUENCE

Influence comes from charisma, expertise, and information. Charisma is a personality trait of compelling charm or attractiveness that can inspire or win other people's devotion or loyalty. Charisma comes from a leader's personality traits or characteristics that others find to be desirable or attractive, such as confidence, ability to speak very well, passion, and humor, among others. Because people find these characteristics desirable or attractive, it's easy for them to follow a charismatic leader.

Expertise is another source of influence, although it has a narrower scope than charisma, as the influence a leader is able to exert on others is limited to the areas of his expertise. Take as an example two guitarists – one classical and the other a rock star.

Classical guitarists, who aren't as popular as rock stars and are known basically for their skills alone, tend to influence other guitar aficionados only to the extent that it will help improve guitar playing. That's influence from expertise.

The rock star guitarist, however, may not be as technically adept as the classical guitarist but, because of his rock star status, he also has influence emanating from his charisma. As such, many of his fans don't just buy the guitars and gears he personally uses – they also mimic the decadent rock and roll lifestyle he lives. His influence transcends his expertise as a guitar player.

So how can you expand or improve your ability to influence people? One is by living true to your core self. People don't follow phony people and not being true to your core will, over time, be found out by others.

Another way to become more influential is to develop your personality, skills, and competencies. Charisma is about personality so, the more confident, positive, calm under pressure, and firm you are, the more people will you find you to be charismatic. Developing your skillsets and competencies will help you become an expert in those fields and can enhance your influence as well owing to your expertise.

POWER OR INFLUENCE?

Alpha males, being socially dominant creatures, are more about influence. This is the reason why women tend to stick to alpha males even if they aren't popular, rich, or powerful, at least politically. This is why gang members are willing to risk their lives for their alpha leaders even without payment. Influence makes people want to do things instead of forcing them to do things. Influence fosters loyalty, which makes people follow you even outside social settings or even if you're not around.

In contrast, power often forces people to follow or obey and it eventually breeds resentment. When people follow you because they have to, all they'll give you is the bare minimum and you can't expect them to go out on a limb for you. Yet that doesn't mean power has no place in an alpha male's life.

There will be times that alpha males need to apply power, particularly coercive power, in order to establish dominance. For example, if a maniac is harassing his lady or a member of his group is being threatened, the alpha will do whatever it takes to protect his woman or his follower. In these situations, he will need to appeal to threats of punishment or very unpleasant experiences to make that maniac or threatening person toe the line and stay away.

Alpha males primarily use influence to lead people and only use power as last resort.

CHAPTER 11

SMART DRESSER

It is both delusional and stupid to think that clothes don't really matter and we should all wear whatever we want. Most people don't take clothing seriously enough, but whether we should or not, clothes do talk to us and we make decisions based on people's appearances. ~G. Bruce Boyer

Do you want a nifty little trick to immediately identify an alpha male while walking down the street or in a mall? Try looking at how the men dress. Do they dress well, so-so, or sloppy? If you see a well-dressed man, then chances are he's alpha.

Alpha males are naturally smart dressers because they value themselves enough to want to look good, not to win people's admiration. They also don't bother themselves with trying to fit in with the other Joes. They are okay to forge their own path and set their own standard. What others do is of little consequence. Others' approval is not a big factor for an alpha. Although being an alpha male makes for smart dressers, one way you can transition into alpha male status is by dressing well.

So how does dressing well help in transitioning into alpha male status?

FIRST IMPRESSIONS

Smart dressing helps make a great first impression...and reinforces such an impression. Without meaning to judge, most of us really evaluate people first by how they look, which seems to be a hardwired program in our minds. It's probably due to evolution. I mean back in the Stone Age, you can't give a saber-tooth tiger the benefit of the adage "don't judge a book by its cover" and think it's too judgmental to think it will eat you for dinner, eh? It's just that even though the threats have been eradicated for the most part, the instinct somehow was continuously passed on to us modern age people.

Whether you like it or not, transitioning into alpha male status requires others' validation – at least in the beginning. In this case dressing well for a great first impression can go a long way toward helping you achieve that goal.

STATUS

Since being an alpha male is a social status, it's important that the people around you perceive you as such. Nothing else screams confidence, character, and ability at first glance than dressing smartly.

How's smart dressing related to character perception? Think of it this way: Dressing smartly requires discipline to learn how to do it and effort and money to pull it off. By dressing smartly, you convey the message that you take the time, effort, and money to make yourself look good and that you value yourself.

CONFIDENCE

Being alpha requires confidence. One way to build up confidence – at least in the beginning – is by dressing well. By exercising control over how you look, you build up your confidence in your ability to control yourself and your situation. When people hold you in high esteem because of how you look, you become more confident in your appearance and as a person. It will eventually snowball and result in a natural confidence in who you really are.

IDENTIFICATION

Let's face it: certain clothing pieces convey status. For example, a doctor's white coat conveys what you do for a living, which happens to be one of the most prestigious professions on earth. A suit and tie conveys the possibility that you're a very prominent or successful man – a lawyer or a CEO of a large company. Dressing smartly identifies you, to a great extent, as an alpha male. Dressing poorly identifies you as omega.

GIVE ORDERS

Since dressing smartly conveys or identifies you as an alpha male, it can also put you in a position where you'll call the shots in most groups. Leadership, at least in the beginning, can be a natural result of smart dressing. Just be careful not rely on smart dressing to continue being an alpha male, all right? It gets you in the door but you'll need more to stay inside.

HOW TO DRESS SMART

Now that you (hopefully) appreciate the value of dressing well, here's how to do it.

First, it's best to start from scratch instead of modifying your existing wardrobe. Remember, your clothes should adjust to who you want to be and not the other way around. This doesn't mean, however, that you should throw everything away in one go! Alpha males don't run around the streets naked, you know!

If budget is a constraint, make it an installment project over a couple of months and discard, as you're able to buy new clothes for your new wardrobe. Just keep in mind how much greater you'd look in your new wardrobe.

ASSUME YOU KNOW NOTHING

Considering your current fashion and that you want to dress smarter, it means whatever it is that you know about smart dressing as of the moment is practically nothing. Therefore, you'll need help in figuring out your new wardrobe.

There are two ways to do this: Hire a fashion consultant, ask fashionable friend to help you out or do your own research. Either way, you get to tap into the minds of those who are experts at looking your best. However, I advise that you do research on your own as a last resort only. The best way to learn how to dress well is through a pair of objective eyes, which is only possible if through a consultant or a friend's eyes.

BACK TO BASICS

Assuming you've ditched everything you know about fashion and have enlisted the services of a friend or a consultant, where should you begin? With the basics, o course!

Getting the basics right alone is already half to three-quarters of the way toward figuring out your new personal fashion style and it practically covers most of your social situations. It's no different from building a house – get the basics first before putting on the accessories.

For the basics, you'll need to buy wardrobe staples that look good in many social situations and can be paired well with just about any piece of clothing like white t-shirts, grey sweaters, and dark blue jeans. Apart from versatility, these can also function as a set of fashion foundation training wheels until you master the basics. Their colors make it fashionably safe for you to experiment with your personal style. Only after you've mastered the basics can you proceed with adding accents and accessories.

KISS (KEEP IT SIMPLE AND SUAVE)

One of the things men take for granted when dressing up is they're not ladies, which means there's little need to be extravagant and for a lot of accessories. Alpha males are the epitome of simple suave and so should you be too. As a famous renaissance man once said, simplicity is the ultimate sophistication.

FIT BEFORE FASHION

If there's a golden rule for dressing well, it's this. No amount of style will make you look good if the clothes are a poor fit. Tight-fitting shirts look good on guys like Ryan Reynolds or Ryan Gosling but would look horrible on chubby guys like Joe Mantegna. Loose-fitting shirts may look cool on Jay-Z on stage but it would look stupid on Hugh Jackman. You get the picture?

So what constitutes a good fit? For shirts, consider the shoulder line. Both lines should rest on your shoulders' edges at the most. If it falls however slightly to your shoulders' sides, the shirt isn't a good fit.

Another way to determine if it's a good fit is how far it drops when un-tucked. If the shirt's edge falls lower than your crotch, it's too long. If it's higher than your crotch, it's too short.

As for pants, if it looks like you're going to a hip-hop convention hosted by Snoop Dogg, then your pants are too big. If your crown jewels feel so snug with each other that your voice becomes high-pitched, you can barely bend your legs and can't sit comfortably in them, they're too tight. Aim for something in between.

DON'T OVERDO IT

Having too many clothes in your new wardrobe can be equally disadvantageous as having too little. If you're building your new wardrobe on a budget, this should be enough to make you do cartwheels.

Resist the temptation to believe that, in this case, the more the merrier. Ever heard of analysis paralysis and information overload? This is what can happen when you have too many clothes in your wardrobe.

In terms of maintaining an ample-sized wardrobe after you've created a new one, periodically check for clothes that either look a bit washed out or don't fit you well anymore. This can help you maintain a right-sized wardrobe that's also current.

MAKE ROOM FOR VARIETY

Lastly, you don't want to be the guy that looks the same day in and day out, month in and month out. Alpha males aren't like that, you know. You need to include variety in your wardrobe.

Note that variety doesn't mean more clothes. It simply means you should buy clothes of different colors or styles, but still within the limits of an ample-sized wardrobe. Include collared, round neck, and dress shirts in your mix as well as a couple of jeans, slacks, and khakis. For footwear, it's always safe to have three pairs, one for formal wear, one for casual wear, and one for athletic wear.

KEEP IT FRESH

Once you have the basics in your collection, and you have developed a solid sense of what works, don't cycle through the same clothes for years to come. Part of what makes this work is a certain level of maintenance. Now relax, I'm not talking about a weekly trip to the mall. That is not necessary. I'm talking about making sure to review what you have every couple of months, seeing if you could use a new item and addressing it. If you do this well for a moment in time, you might fit the alpha status. But if you let it slide a few months, then it's all for not. Don't let your clothes get worn and don't wait so long to buy new things that your look is outdated. If you only invest in a few new outfits, and you cycle through them every few days, your look can get tired. Avoid this for your own benefit. Continue to take pride in your look. There is no point in going to the gym and getting fit just to start a cheesecake diet and quit the gym just as soon as the abs are starting to show through. It works the same with your wardrobe. Don't let it get stale. Keep it up. Get interested in trends. Prioritize fit but also be a little bold at times.

CHAPTER 12

THE SCIENCE OF ATTRACTION TO ALPHAS

What do girls and women all around the world want in a perfect guy? A tall, dark, handsome man with gentlemanly qualities, who will treat them like princesses, someone who is strong and silent, who will fight for them if need be, kind, intelligent, and loyal to them. All the good things in one package, right?

But, sad as it is true, no one man possesses all these qualities. And most of the womenfolk out there might have dated someone who does not fit any of the criteria mentioned above. Or, they perhaps even discounted someone who did display the traits. It's actually quite confusing, this science of attraction. What makes someone tick and what doesn't? An attractive quality in one might be anathema for another.

The Myth of the Alpha Male

As we have read till now, any males who are at the top of the social hierarchy, with greater access to status, power, money, and show, are classified as alpha males. They are physically imposing, intimidating, and appealing. Often described as the big men or the real men, they make the betas and omegas look like weaklings. Who would look at a nice, submissive guy, keeping to himself, occasionally surfacing to meet people, talking in a soft voice? These guys are classified as the nice guys or the losers whom the women approach when they have no other choices left.

But is this distinction correct? Or are we guilty of painting an extremely black and white picture? Both masculinity and femininity are incredibly complex aspects of personality, and a mere listing of traits and characteristics does grossly underestimate the actual capacity of a man or a woman.

The point here is this: every human being (whether male or female) on this planet has both the characteristics of masculinity and femininity. Only the proportion changes to make a man manly and a woman womanly. We do see plenty of women who are tomboyish and also men who are feminine, although the latter category is mocked upon and the former is applauded. Femininity is naturally drawn toward emotions; that's just the way the blueprint was intended to be. Early females had to be extremely attuned to their environment as well as the emotions and needs of those around them in order to survive and provide good care to their offspring and family. The male only had to bring in the kill and relax by the fire. It was the female who nurtured and provided warmth, care, and love and kept her senses sharp enough to sense mood and emotion changes around her. Nothing much has changed in thousands of years. Men are still unidirectional, women multidirectional. And this is the reason why women are much better at expressing emotions than men. It's not as if the males don't feel any emotion. They just don't know how to express it.

They've never been conditioned that way. And it's more so with the alpha males, who have a macho image to portray at all times.

The Attraction to the Alpha Male

Females everywhere want to date a macho man. Even the most intelligent and discerning of them manage to fall for the alpha male, the top guy. The sweet gentleman, who brings them small gifts, massages their feet, listens to their problems, and offers solutions might be a great catch on paper, but he just doesn't score when it comes to the raw, sensual appeal the alpha male exudes to others. The gentleman is too one-dimensional, as opposed to the dark and dangerous world of the alpha male. This is why we see Casanovas, the top guys, the "bad guys" roaming around with smart, bright women who themselves have no clue why they are going along with them. All logic is put aside and the hormones win the game.

Why it is that women never want what's good for them? Are they genetically predisposed to find darker personalities more appealing? Of course, females know that such men will sooner or later break their hearts and go out with dozens of girls at the same time, but somehow they are unable to resist the charm of the bad boy. A study conducted by Gregory Louis Carter of the University of Durham tried to peek into this weird and vexing world. The research revealed that the traits of narcissism, Machiavellianism, and psychopathy, often known as the Dark Triad, were found more abundantly in men than in women. And these complementary traits lead women to find such alpha men alluring and fascinating, even at the cost of their own happiness and sanity.

Men who own the room, the conversation, and the power-packed business lunch are generally perceived as mentally and physically strong, with masculine energy just flowing out of them. No wonder that the contrasting feminine energy finds them so tempting.

We've all been there. Seen it on television, in the movies. Read about it in books. The bad boy reputation of being enormously hot, rugged, scruffy, with a body to die for, an arrogant and a slightly condescending attitude, sometimes inconsiderate as well. But women flock to them in droves. They hang onto their every word. Studies conducted with 500 women subjects on this topic have revealed some interesting insights. Apparently, women are attracted toward the macho guys and the bad boys due to their rocky relationships with their parents, particularly their fathers. As little girls, they never got the love and attention of their fathers, the primary male figure in their lives, and ended up kissing a lot of frogs in order to get to their princes. Another aspect is that women tended to look upon such guys as grown-up children, spoiled, bratty, scruffy, untidy, yet extremely charming and open. They believed that they could change them into good people. This mothering instinct showed up in more than 80% of the respondents. This study threw up three major factors of "bad boy attraction."

1. Amazing sex: The number one reason on the list. But the "look" of the macho man was also an important consideration here. Women were shown different male looks and asked to judge potential mates on the basis of their faces. Men with chiseled, square jaws, defined ridges of the brow, and a sharp nose were preferred over rounder faces, with fuller lips. The latter category was more suited for long-term mates.

2. The challenge: What challenge? Convert a bad boy into a loving, caring and supportive mate. Women are hardwired for maternal instincts and they fervently believed that the bad boys could be changed. Needless to say, that never happens.

3. The thrill: Dating a macho guy or a bad boy is totally against the set rules and norms of society. Hard-core criminals, rugged-looking macho men, wild cowboys were out of reach, mentally and physically for the women. So doing something against the rules was a huge thrill for them.

An important biological fact to be kept in mind: Female hormones make them choose bad boys, according to research. During ovulation, certain hormones come into play that make the women pick rugged, more masculine looking and sexier men as partners, regardless of their social status. Whether or not they choose to pursue a long-term relationship with such men is entirely open to debate.

But, as always, there is a downside to this. Dating an alpha male can be an exhausting process. He is obsessed with himself, trying to up the ante all the time, jealously guarding his position, controlling those around him, and he can even be demeaning and violent. As we have discussed, monogamy is not a very attractive proposition in evolutionary terms. The alpha male is more prone to philandering. He does this consciously as well, because he is aware of his raw appeal, his darker side that draws women to him like a magnet.

Alpha males are emotional beings. They are passionate about everything they do and put all their efforts into them. Normally, the alphas are great partners, giving and loving and caring. But the hitch here is this: They expect as much as they give and when they don't receive emotions and feelings in equal proportion, that's when the problems begin. Any small thing can trigger a negative response in them and, when it does, it completely clouds their judgment. This impulse control disorder is only a personality flaw and certainly not a serious mental problem. If this continues for a longer period of time, say months or years, it is transformed into a habit that may be hard to break.

CHAPTER 13

HE'S A CHALLENGE TO WOMEN

If you say to a woman "I really like you", it won't be as effective as saying to them "You really like me" in a teasing way. ~ David Dingell

Women, according to dating guru David DeAngelo, are generally attracted to a man who is:

-In control of himself;

-In control of his situations; and

-In control of them (the women).

An alpha male can do what he wants and needs to do because he's confident of his skills and abilities, his values and beliefs, and who he is. He therefore exercises a great deal of self-control, which is his gateway to controlling or influencing others. Can you imagine someone who has little to no self-control being able to control their situations and other people? I doubt it.

An alpha male is also able – to a great extent – to control his situations or surroundings. Through this, he demonstrates or communicates power, strength, and ability – traits that many people find attractive, especially women. It especially communicates confidence that's backed up by reality.

Lastly, women subconsciously want or desire men who are able to control them, according to DeAngelo. It's because, deep inside, women are wired to desire being taken care of and pursued. By being able to make women feel he's in control, an alpha male makes it hard for women not to be attracted to him.

BE A CHALLENGE

The key to communicating to women that you're in control, and thus an alpha male, is by challenging them. Why? Consider the economic principle of supply and demand, which states that the perceived value of an object is directly proportional to its availability. Simply put, the scarcer a thing is, the more valuable and desirable it becomes.

Consider a diamond and a piece of coal. Both are primarily composed of carbon, but why are diamonds so expensive and coal, well, so cheap? It's because diamonds are harder to find compared to coal.

How does this relate to women? Especially the hot ones, women are used to having guys falling at their feet, desperately trying to earn their affection. Over time, this becomes something that's expected of most men.

Natural selection dictates women choose the best possible mating partner from among the multitudes of men available. If most men behave the same, i.e., fall at women's feet and worship them in hopes of winning their love (or loins), it makes such a choice difficult because all men then become the same. There's an oversupply of needy and easy-to-manipulate men and, if you approach women as such, you automatically get labeled as ordinary or not worth their time and affection...or loins.

But if you prove to be quite a challenge to her, you immediately separate yourself from the pack and serve notice that you're not ordinary. You're different – you're the best.

HOW TO BE CHALLENGING

There are many ways to be challenging enough to women but in general, it can be summed up this way: never give her exactly what she wants. According to David DeAngelo, this means not being her puppy dog who's at her beck and call, but this also doesn't mean you should always do the opposite of what she wants. What this means is that when you indulge her requests, you shouldn't give them to her exactly the way she wants it. For example, if she wants to watch the X-Men tomorrow evening, you can either:

-Watch the movie with her on some other day of your choice; or

-Watch another movie with her tomorrow evening.

Another way of doing this is by having the balls to tease her like you would your younger sister. Why? Since most men worship her to high heavens, they tend to be on the safe side and don't say anything risky like making a joke out of her hair or the clothes she's wearing. They don't have the balls to risk offending her. That's why she's bored to death with nice guys!

When you kiddingly tease her about, say her hair that resembles a burning bush in a way that's funny, you subtly tell her two things: You're not afraid of her and you're confident about yourself enough that you don't need her approval. When she sees you're not afraid of her, she senses you are able to control yourself, the situation between you and her and even her! And these three things are what women want in men, remember?

As an alpha male, you should challenge your woman constantly in a good and healthy way by not giving her exactly what she wants and by having the balls to kiddingly tease her like you would your kid sister. As you do that, you make see you as someone who's in control of yourself, your situation, and even her. And that's what will make her be attracted to you, the alpha male of her life.

CHAPTER 14

THE LAWS OF MANLINESS

You can learn a lot by reading books written by or about great men. They tell you about success stories of the amazing men in the history of humans, and how they came to be so great. If you read books like *The Rise of Napoleon Bonaparte*, *Rise of Theodore Roosevelt*, and *Robert E. Lee on Leadership*, you will learn so much about true manliness that you can't imagine. You will want to emulate these personalities, and it will help you become an even better alpha. Chapter 15 showcases some great alphas.

In today's time, where masculinity is on the decline and there's a war being fought against masculine values, it's important that we bring back the old values and stick to them. The society fears masculine values because it doesn't understand them, and that is why we're losing our strength. We're becoming more and more corruptible by the day. We're becoming incredibly self-entitled and have started to rely too much on others. That is not how a real man behaves. We need to bring back real strength.

Men used to be warriors and protectors, and that's what we need to become again. We need to protect ourselves and our societies from evil, and that requires strength, both of body, and of spirit. It will serve us well in all areas of life. You must have the courage of David, the strength of Leonidas, the boldness of Caesar. You need to embody the cherished values of manliness. And for this reason, I bring to you *The Laws of Manliness*.

1. Be self-reliant.

It's a quickly disappearing quality among men, and this trend is worrying. There's a growing sense of entitlement among people that makes us feel like we deserve the things we haven't earned yet. Don't accept the life of dependency. Sustain yourself, and never look for a handout. This doesn't mean you can never ask for help. You can, and you should when you really need it, but that shouldn't be your default mode of thinking. Always repay the help you receive from someone.

You can seek guidance when you need it but, to be truly self-reliant, you need to be in control of your success, your future, and your happiness. Never give that power to someone else. Be the rock others lean on, not the other way around.

See yourself as the source of your life. Live from this perspective. Go get what it is you want. The idea that good things come to those that wait is rarely true. It often works as good things come to people who keep their eye on the prize and work smart toward what they want. Along the way you may need to remind yourself to stay the course and be patient but "waiting" is not part of a great life.

2. Understand that success and happiness require hard work.

Never think that you're born into success. You always have to work for it and earn your success. Success and happiness in life don't come easy, whether you're talking about your professional life or your personal life. You have to work for them.

Don't believe the delusion that success is your birthright or that there's any other way to achieve it besides hard work. Hold a strong resolve at all times and hustle until you achieve your goals. Don't look for shortcuts to grueling problems. Sometimes the only way to the other side is directly through, not around. The taste of victory is much sweeter when it's actually earned. Take control of your destiny and drive it.

Also, remember that hard work does not mean pouring all of your energies into something, losing balance and not recognizing signs of changing course. This is where you add together working smart and working hard. Definitely be willing to put your energy in, however, also be smart about where you spend your time. If you're an entrepreneur, and you know you have great strengths in an aspect of your business, spend your energy wisely in that realm. If you can hire out other parts of the workload or train yourself to be more effective in those other aspects, now that is working smart. Banging your head against a wall and getting mediocre outcomes does not create success.

3. *Practice self-denial and forget about instant gratification.*

We're born into a generation that is always seeking instant gratification. We have our credit cards and loans and whatnot. It's become much easier to buy things we don't need to impress people we don't even like or even know. This attitude must change.

Read about any great man and you will see self-denial as a common trait among them. They don't crave instant gratification. They seek to constantly improve themselves and become better men by denying themselves easy pleasures. They have the long term in mind, the end game.

So identify things that hinder your growth and then remove them from your life one at a time. Replace them with things that actually help you go forward in life. It doesn't matter what they are. Whether you watch too much TV or consume too much junk food, take control of your life and deny yourself these things. Taking a moment to check yourself on these vices also strengthens your mind. These small feats you take on concerning your personal habits can easily build your willpower, and that can help you make better business decisions. For example, take the larger picture into account.

4. Forge your own path. Don't be afraid to dream of a big life.

This one, despite being a tricky law, is very important. You have to do a lot of trials by error before you find the right path for yourself, the thing you really want to do, and the kind of man you want to become. But it's important that you do so.

You *will* fail multiple times, but the only way to do so is by stepping into the arena and trying. You will constantly face your greatest fears and conquer them, because that's what it takes to be a real man. You have to be the guy who is still training in the gym long after everyone else has left, the guy who has the ball at the end of the game, the last man standing in the ring. So go out, step into the arena, and don't be afraid to do the work others aren't willing to do. It's the only way to surpass others.

5. Don't be afraid to fight, even if you may lose. Never throw someone else under the bus for your own mistakes.

Many of us are so used to living an easy life that the idea of a hard life scares us. But to rise above others, you have to defeat these fears. Don't fear living the life of an eternal warrior; it's the only way people will remember you. Teddy Roosevelt was a fighter, and so was Napoleon, but we shouldn't include only the ones who were fighters in the literal sense. Jobs was a fighter, too, and so was Gandhi.

I have met so many men who have never been in a real fight. It makes them cowards because they don't dare to go beyond their fears. You don't have to be careless, but if something you care about is in peril, like your honor or your lady, go forth and fight for it. Never turn your back on your values, even if that's not what others believe in. Fight for them. It's an important thing for a real man.

6. *Accept responsibility for your actions. Go out of the way to take the blame.*

The biggest defining characteristic of a coward is that he never sees his own fault. He always blames his failures on someone else. In this time, when honor is a fast-disappearing trait, it is the mark of a real man to own up to his mistakes. The vast majority of people no longer accept their mistakes. They always find an excuse, a way to deflect the blame to someone else.

Let's take the example of two leaders: Barack Obama and Robert E. Lee.

If you put everything else aside and just focus on their character, you can notice how different the two of them are as leaders. Lee, a product of his own time, was still better than his peers. He lived by strong values and revered honor. His principles were deep founded and he was an original man. Obama, on the other hand, is full of vanity, a growing trait among men of today. He never accepts blame for anything.

Lee accepted blame for anything wrong that happened under his command, even when he was not directly responsible for it. He would always take it in stride to work on the mistake and see it taken care of. Obama never accepts any of the blame and refuses to take a stand like a strong man should. Most men in our time are like this, and we need to change that. We need people of Lee's integrity, people who have strong principles and values.

You cannot call yourself a man unless you are a man of honor.

7. Don't be afraid to stand alone on your principles and values.

A real man doesn't need numbers to support himself. He has strength within himself to stand firmly for his values. Only the weak need numbers because they are cowardly and can't stand on their principles.

You shouldn't be attention-seeking. Our society is heading toward a future in which everyone is dependent on what others think of them, and it alters our thinking. We need to feel accepted and it taints our actions. If you want to be a true leader, walk to the beat of your own tune, and think for yourself. Be original and don't give in to the need to feel accepted by others.

True leaders of history have always had their originality, their uniqueness, both in thought and in action. That is not to say that they were not influenced by others, but that they made their own decisions after careful thinking and original insight. That is what we all should strive to be. Be your own man, and stick to creating a true identity for yourself.

8. Don't be afraid to fail. Be far more afraid of never trying.

You know what a coward does? He never tries because he is afraid to fail. If you want to talk game, be sure you act on it. Don't make empty boasts among your friends and then step back. That's cowardly, and something a real man should never do. Talk less, do more. If something doesn't need to be said, it doesn't need to be said. People don't respect you for how eloquent you speak. They see your actions and are intrigued or possibly inspired. An alpha male acts on his words and leaves a legacy for others to follow. He doesn't shy away from failure. He sees it as a natural part of eventual success. He learns from it. He shares it without regret. More important, he immediately moves on to bigger and better things. He is built up by the challenges he encounters. He grows in the face of problems. He does not shrink.

9. *Practice kindness, but not weakness.*

"Give a man a fish and you feed him for a day. Teach a man to fish and you will feed him for a lifetime."

If you have a skill, teach it to others, because that's what people ultimately need. It's common for people these days to just throw money at their problems. But that's not a real solution. You should give your mind and your time to a problem, not just money.

Money can indeed be incredibly useful in the hands of the right person. You can use it for charities, for building schools and hospitals. Giving your money to those who really need it, for things that make a difference, that's noble. But it shouldn't be a way out of difficult situations for you.

Always be kind and help others, but be thoughtful too. Think about things and make a decision after due diligence. Being weak is not the same thing as being kind, so actually make an effort to know things. You should carry yourself, not want others to carry you. Every man wants to carry himself, and if you can find a way to give him that power, that's the biggest kindness you can show him.

10. Never turn a blind eye to injustice. Never walk past someone in need of your help.

Men have protected their tribes and their people for thousands of years, from beasts, from nature, and from other men. That's not how the world works anymore, but that doesn't mean you should give up these ways so quickly. You should still be protective of people, especially those who are facing injustice. The world is a mean place filled with evil people who don't think twice before harming others. You should never turn a blind eye to this sort of injustice.

It is your duty to protect your family, your friends, and even strangers who are too weak to fend for themselves. Stand up against injustice and defend people who are vulnerable. It hurts a lot when you're in need of help and you see people walking past you without sparing you another look. As Martin Luther King Jr. put it, "In the end, we will remember not the words of our enemies, but the silence of our friends."

The world is going to the dogs, my friends. Helpless people get acid thrown in their faces, get raped and mugged in shady street corners. The poor keep getting poorer, and children are taken advantage of by predators. People are slaughtered in the name of religion, and people abuse their position of power to get ill-gotten gains. We shouldn't stand by idly as all of this happens. We should raise our voices and stand up against it.

Never be afraid to stand against the majority. Even if there's an army in front of you and nothing but the wind behind your back, you must stand your ground against injustice. Don't cower in the face of danger.

11. Read as much as you can.

Spend considerable time reading. Read about everything, including not just people who inspire you, but also those whose worldview differs from yours. It is the mark of a smart person to be able to entertain an idea without accepting it or agreeing with it. If you happen to be a liberal, read something written by a conservative, and deeply think about it, and vice versa. If you're a deeply religious person, read something written by an atheist. Read about science, economics, business, sports, everything. Learn about different cultures and politics. Most of the best conversationalists and the most amazing thinkers I know are constantly devouring new knowledge. They are not threatened by something that sounds contrary to their current beliefs. They can sometimes be attracted to it. They learn how their opponents think. They become worldlier by being able to see different angles. Reading is a gift, and you can learn more than you can imagine from it. So get out of your comfort zone often and just *read*! A little hint to make this doable in a busy schedule is to get audio books. There are tons of great apps to choose from. Make the most of your exercise or commute by listening to an audiobook. Each day you can expand your mind a bit more.

12. Be just and fair.

Our idea of fairness is constantly being bastardized and diluted. This is because honorable qualities are disappearing from the society, and a growing number of people want what they haven't earned. It's the mentality of the weak. Yes, some people need and deserve our help, and it's on us to help them. But you should never envy another man's possessions. It's dangerous and unmanly to do so. Don't expect someone else to give you a part of what they have simply because you think you didn't have the same opportunities in life. That's weakness.

Admit that life isn't fair and that's how it's always going to be until the end of time. If you want something, work for it and leave no stone unturned in your quest to be successful. It is in your hands to make your life what you want it to be.

13. Unplug weekly.

We become disconnected from our values and our mission when we get too lost in the noise of everyday life. Our beliefs and intentions become clouded, and we lose sight of our purpose. Silence is golden, and it can be your most valuable friend in life. We need it to reconnect with ourselves and to our purpose. It gives us clarity, and it is in silence that we recharge. We rediscover ourselves and hear our doubts and fears clearly. When we stop pacifying ourselves with the quick enjoyment and distractions that our busy lives provide, we learn to be with ourselves. We become present to what matters and are able to better prioritize.

That is why it's very important to unplug yourself from everyday activities at least once a week. It helps you hear your own thoughts and keep your purpose clear.

14. Don't live on the Internet.

With the advent of social media and all the garbage we're fed on the interwebs, it has become very difficult to maintain real, physical interaction with people. We have allowed ourselves to become an online persona, someone who lives on the Internet, and this has affected how we deal with things in the real life.

On the Internet, we can control what we show people. We don't have to give them the complete story and we can choose to show them only part of who we are, which is dangerous. It changes how we gain meaning for our lives. We start caring more about what others think of us on the Internet, and life becomes all about changing profile pictures and updating statuses, showing people where we've been, and what we've been reading. It has become almost a competition. The relationships we have with people have become virtual.

If you want to be a real man, don't live on the Internet. Ground yourself in the reality of the physical world, and don't get caught up in what people think of you on Facebook. Don't worry about the number of "likes" on your photos or how many "friends" you have. These things don't matter, and your real friends will stay in contact with you despite Facebook. Show the world who you really are.

15. Be chivalrous.

Chivalry is dying, and fast. There are many reasons, one of which is that men no longer want to go the extra mile. They just don't care enough to do chivalrous deeds, and chivalry is not being taught to them anymore. But it is important for a real man to be chivalrous. A good man lives by this code and always follows it.

16. Have a grand adventure at least once in your life.

I had always wanted to visit India because I had heard so much about it. Last year, I suddenly realized that I was single and had full freedom to go anywhere and work from there. I had been living in the same place all my life, so I decided to go on a grand adventure and booked a three-month trip to India. It was one of the most fulfilling things I've ever done in my life, and it required me to take *action*! You also need to take action to have a great adventure at least once in your life.

If you're planning to go on a long trip to a foreign land, here are some tips:

1) Have a good credit card. You might not realize it but soon, in a couple of years hopefully, you will have enough points to book most of your entire trip.

2) Don't stay in a hotel. You can't expect to shell out hundreds of dollars every day if you want to stay for an extended period. Instead, you should try something like Airbnb or Couchsurfing. It's much cheaper that way and you can still earn some money all that while doing freelance work. You can easily make friends via Couchsurfing and stay with them, or if that doesn't seem good enough to you, you can use Airbnb to get good places for as low as $500 a month. If you don't want to have a very lavish lifestyle on your trip, definitely check out Airbnb.

3) Don't be afraid. Do whatever you truly want to do and go anywhere without fear of getting lost or stranded. It will help you improve your survival skills and make you a stronger man.

17. Laugh daily, and don't take yourself too seriously.

Life is nothing without joy, and you need to loosen up at times in order to really enjoy life. All of the real men I know, whether living or dead, know not to take themselves too seriously and laugh a lot. They have a good sense of humor, which everyone appreciates. They also don't mind laughing at themselves.

So it's important for you to learn how to not take yourself too seriously and be able to make fun of yourself at times. It helps you loosen up and enjoy life more. You will work harder as a result and accomplish more.

We all have our own flavor of weirdness and little idiosyncrasies that make us unique, and we can use this uniqueness to be funny. Humor is the best way to bring together two opposite sides. So at times, it's okay to be the butt of a joke. You can use humor to defuse the tension in almost any situation, and it can also give you insights into the absurdities of life sometimes.

A man who can laugh at himself is as secure in himself as he can be.

18. Speak with your actions, not with your words.

A real man talks less and does more. It's not your words that make you a big man; it's your actions. You should be the embodiment of toughness, humility, and pride. Vanity and envy shouldn't even come close to you. John Wayne wanted to portray the qualities of a real man in all of his silver screen characters because that is what he wanted to inspire the younger generation to be.

Men in movies today seldom have these qualities. They don't act as much as they talk, and that is why society is losing these qualities as a whole. Respect the weight of every word that comes out of your mouth and don't waste your breath on useless talk. Be the type of man who chooses his words wisely and is firm in his actions.

19. *Be the best at what you do.*

To become your best, you have to *attempt* to be at your best at all times. Life isn't about merely existing, so whatever you do, do it with all of your heart. Give it your 100%. Never accept mediocrity, and always aspire to go beyond what others can do. Whatever you do in life, aspire to be the best, both in professional and personal endeavors.

20. *Don't chase money, find meaning.*

In your vision of a good life, material things shouldn't be on the top of your list. If you have a huge wish list with motorbikes and cars and huge mansions on it, you're not doing it right. They're trivial, and you will later realize that the most important thing is to find meaning in life. Your pride in yourself should be because of the things you *do*, not because of what you own.

So make sure you have a solid mission and work toward its fulfillment. Don't live for a paycheck. Go out and live for meaning, for an adventure you will never forget. Create an identity for yourself and make a mark for yourself. Buy yourself nice things, but remember how insignificant they really are in the greater scheme of life.

21. Make the best out of every situation.

A real man makes the best out of every situation, no matter how bad it seems. Robert E. Lee is one such type of man who made the best out of everything, and that is one of the reasons why he is remembered so dearly. No matter how dark a situation seems, be the person who switches on the light, be the one who provides hope to those who have none left. Never wish to live someone else's life, and always learn from your mistakes. It will ultimately help you lead a meaningful life. And that is the way of a real man, a warrior, an alpha.

CHAPTER 15

REAL LIFE ALPHA MEN AND LESSONS TO LEARN FROM THEM

Hugh Hefner

We've all heard of Hugh Hefner, the staunch libertarian who has always been against restriction on sexuality. Regardless of whether you agree to his views or not, you have to admit that his confidence in expressing them is admirable and certainly ahead of his time. In one of his high school essays, he attacked America's Puritanism, and in another term paper in grad school, he praised the Kinsey report, *Sexual Behavior in the Human Male*.

Lesson: Personal convictions don't equate to personal restrictions.

Personal beliefs are often regarded by others as restrictive but, for a true alpha male, that's not the case. He lives life on his own terms and according to his own convictions, but that doesn't mean he lets them put him at a disadvantage. Instead, he uses them as a guide to his success. You can see that in Hugh Hefner's decision to launch *Playboy*, a magazine that promotes his beliefs and shows his ability to obtain results from it. He didn't passively sit behind his beliefs. He put them to some use.

Douglas MacArthur

Douglas MacArthur did three different tours of duty prior to the Second World War, and had a longstanding association with the Philippines. He was made the commander of Philippines in 1941, responsible for defending the islands from the Japanese for the Allies. When the Japanese forces attacked, he was able to hold them off for a long time. He slowly retreated to the Bataan Peninsula and didn't give up until President Roosevelt insisted that he should flee to Australia. After the army's surrender to the Japanese, his soldiers suffered horribly as prisoners of war, and that's when MacArthur vowed to return.

MacArthur never lost sight of this and he delivered on his promise three years later. He reclaimed the entire Commonwealth but, more than that, he got the ultimate revenge. In 1945, he was personally present to accept the surrender of the Japanese forces aboard USS Missouri.

Lesson: When you make a promise, always deliver on it.

If you're all talk, nobody will ever respect you. There aren't many other traits more unappealing than this. People who make empty promises come to be known as unreliable and impotent. You don't want to be that guy, so you should always deliver on your promises. And remember never to promise the impossible.

John Wayne

John Wayne, born Marion Robert Morrison, will always be known as an American icon, The Duke. He was such an iconic figure, in fact, that when the Japanese emperor Hirohito was visiting the US in the 1970s, he specifically asked to meet Wayne. He had this rugged tough-guy persona that commanded respect, and he inspired many men to enlist for military service despite the fact that he never technically served himself. He insisted on maintaining his image until the very end, wanting his characters to stay away from anything ignoble, like shooting a man in the back.

That is why he had such a powerful presence as a man, most of which was because of something very simply: posture. Most of us take it for granted, but it's worth paying attention to. Unlike many others, John Wayne never slouched. He would always keep his back straight and his shoulders cocked. He never overdid it, and because of this, he had an imposing presence wherever he went.

Lesson: Don't underestimate the power of presence.

Wayne was always the most badass man in the room, and yes, I know we all can't be tall, handsome, ass-kicking movie stars. But the important lesson to learn here is how to carry yourself. Wayne always had a body language and demeanor that commanded respect. You see, people tend to read body language all the time, even at a subconscious level. If you slouch or hunch your shoulders during an important meeting or a similar situation, you can lose the confidence of your peers quickly. Remember that how people perceive you is important. If you give an impression of strength, people will respect you and regard you as powerful.

Muhammad Ali

If you've ever watched a match of the great Muhammad Ali, you know how smart a trash-talker he was, possibly the best in the history of sports. He was indeed one of the greatest boxers ever, but he was also a master of self-promotion. He would always be tremendously confident in himself, so much so that his charisma would intimidate his opponents. He would often predict the round in which his opponent would be knocked out.

Ali would often proclaim to be the greatest ever, and this bragging routine seemed like nervous bravado to his opponents during the early days of his career. In reality, however, it was his preparation that made him feel so superior. Those who knew him had complete faith in him, because they knew how hard he trained and how indomitable his will was. Ali pushed himself so hard that he had every reason to believe he was invincible in the ring. He was sure he had pushed himself beyond what any other man could sustain.

Lesson: Always come prepared.

Alphas never step into an important situation without preparation, regardless of what impression they give off. They never take their abilities for granted. So if you really, *really* want to win, never delude yourself by thinking you're already good enough. Push yourself beyond your limits and be prepared in all circumstances.

Say, you're supposed to give the toast at the wedding of your best friend. It may seem harmless to go unprepared. After all, you're a confident public speaker and you know your best friend so well, right? You don't know how wrong you are. Whatever you may think, you *will* fumble and say something dumb in the middle of your toast, simply because you thought you were too good to prepare. If you want to be an alpha male, always prepare with intensity and leave nothing to chance.

Gordon Ramsay

As we all know, Gordon Ramsay is one of the most celebrated chefs in the whole world. Michelin, the industry's most prominent ratings guide, has awarded his restaurants three starts 10 times! Yes, that's right. But, ironically, Ramsay himself has no interest in being liked by others. He doesn't want to be the winner of a popularity contest. If you've ever seen him work on "Hell's Kitchen," you know what I'm talking about.

He's a brutal taskmaster, completely indifferent to the feelings of people and only cares about results. He doesn't care if you like him, but he demands your respect as a chef. It may sound surprising, but he has a staff retention rate of 85% since 1993. You may be wondering why people don't leave if he's such a hard taskmaster.

Lesson: Do not accept mediocrity.

There's one simple reason why Ramsay's employees don't leave: they know he's the best. They all want to be the best at their craft, and no matter what Ramsay's flaws are, they know that, in the end, he pushes them all to be the best. It's not difficult to realize that compared to all the great achievements, his abuse is just trivial. He doesn't tolerate mediocrity in his professional life, and that's what you should learn from him. Always weed out the weak links and strengthen your team by removing all doubts from people's minds. It boosts the team's confidence.

Napoleon Bonaparte

The famous Frenchman, emperor and military leader, totes a phenomenal history of conquering much of Europe. He certainly didn't wait around for opportunities to be handed to him. He was driven and was taking what he wanted. He organized a coup in 1799 that landed him the supreme leader of France and then gave himself the crown for the emperor in 1804. He was determined and marched straight to what he wanted. It wasn't all show either. He was extremely skilled at military strategy. His military leadership wasn't without hiccups. He was exiled not once but twice. Don't forget all of his wins, though. He didn't let a couple of bumps in the road (we're talking major bumps) slow him down. His determination lived on.

Lesson: Don't get stopped.

When roadblocks arise, the tendency may be to take a new path or turn around. You might even say "well, I tried." Don't sell yourself out like that. People like Napoleon faced major barriers but kept their focus. They pulled themselves up by their bootstraps and kept going. Alphas do not get stopped when someone says "no." They may look at the situation and analyze what makes the most sense. But they never let what is easiest be the driver for their action. Their convictions come first. If they decide a roadblock must be overcome, they rally their people and their resources to make it happen.

Alexander the Great

Before the age of thirty, Alexander the Great was moving mountains. Through his military wizardry, he had established an empire so large it was among the biggest in the world. What have most 30 year-olds accomplished today? He may have been born into a powerful family, but he didn't use his status to take a free ride. He constantly pushed the envelope. As the king of the ancient Greek kingdom of Macedon, he honed his military skills and strategies so much so that he was studied and emulated for years to come.

Lesson: Carve your own path.

Even though Alexander the Great could have sat back and done a modest amount of work to maintain a good life, he did not accept that. He wanted to make a mark in the world that was bold and distinct from what his father had done. Some people today are born into money and privilege. They know they can get away with a comfortable life by just leeching off of their families and close circles. This is no life. It is certainly a waste of the potential the alpha man can bring to this world. Even if you were born into a comfortable life, it doesn't mean you need to maintain the status quo. Being comfortable is not the thing in life that will bring you satisfaction. It also has little positive impact on anyone else. Think about the person you want to be in this world. Do you want to make a mark? An American take on a Lancashire proverb is "Shirt sleeves to shirt sleeves in three generations." This means that people who attain wealth will provide it to their children and before you know it, the drive to work and achieve may be lost, and then all of the wealth is gone, and the family line is right back where it started...in shirtsleeves (meaning a working man). Even if there is a family business, put your own mark on it. Add in something new. Brand yourself distinct from where you came from.

Franklin Roosevelt

FDR is an American legend and no surprise, he's also an alpha. He not only helped America rise to power, but he led the country through WWII. No one envied the work he had to do, but they saw his wisdom and strong will in action. He was well-admired. He was decisive and powerful. He had the tough job of leading the country through the Great Depression as well. Things may have been a lot worse had he not taken the actions he did and made the hard decisions. He led people and inspired them to act. On the personal side of things, he got polio and became paralyzed in both legs. It was after this that he campaigned for and became president. He was unstoppable. He was principled. He was quoted as having said, "If you could kick the person in the pants responsible for most of your trouble, you wouldn't sit for a month." He also said, "With self-discipline almost anything is possible."

Lesson: You are the one responsible for the change.

Roosevelt, like other admirable alphas, did not see the external world as being responsible for the change he wanted to see. He took it upon himself to make things happen. He looked to himself to be the leader. He held himself responsible for things working out or failing. That responsible viewpoint gave him a perspective of being powerful and also needed. He called on himself to do what needed to be done. He stepped up. He had every excuse to step back and take it easy. He ended up being elected three times as president. He knew there was still work to do. He didn't do it for the glory. He had conviction. An alpha sees themselves as critical to any change or process. This is not a matter of being self-centered or overly obsessed with oneself. It is a matter of being willing to take responsibility for the good and the bad. Alphas don't sit around and complain about the way things are. They become the source of the solution.

Dr. Martin Luther King Jr.

Few would argue that Dr. King was a bold leader. Think about the key characteristics of an alpha male. He was bold. He didn't wait for other's permission or look to others for approval. He was strong-willed and determined. He commanded a room, hell, a crowd...really, a movement. He was steadfast in his beliefs and confident in himself. Let's not deny he was also skilled with women and as charismatic as they come. His "I have a dream....." speech is known all over the world. He certainly did. He was a founder of modern America if you will. He transformed a country. He changed the dialogue. He challenged a lot of people to see things differently.

Lesson: Dare to dream big.

Dr. King didn't shy away from making strong declarations. When people doubted things would change, he spoke louder. His tactics were not always gentle. He arranged for demonstrations that would draw a crowd and more importantly, draw attention. Lots of people asked him to stop. Many times his life was even threatened. He did not have a consensus behind him, but his vision was clear. He dared to dream big, announce it to the world and then go for it with everything he had.

Nelson Mandela

Although he needs no introduction, Nelson Mandela ranks among the most influential in modern history. He moved a nation, a continent, and the world to challenge their assumptions and norms about race. To say he radically moved a nation to reconsider apartheid would be an understatement. He put his whole life on the line to transform South Africa. The country today is unrecognizable in comparison to its former ways. Although nothing is perfect, people of color have access to government services, education, rights, jobs and all that is available to white people. At the time Mandela was taking a lead in the anti-apartheid movement, this was not the inevitable future. If things had gone the way they were going, the country would look entirely different today. Much more people of color would have suffered and even died. He transformed that.

Lesson: Don't be afraid of a lofty challenge.

When things are bad, alphas step up to take the reins. It's not an easy job. It may often be a thankless job, but someone bold has to do it. That would be the alphas. They see things that have great potential yet also great challenges and start building a vision. They move into action to make an impact. They stand for themselves, their values and other people. Most importantly, they stand for what they know to be right. In the face of a lot of uncertainty and also a lot of dissent, they stand strong. That is the true mark of an alpha.

CHAPTER 16

ARE YOU AN ALPHA MALE OR A BULLY?

There's a fine line between being an alpha male and being a bully, in much the same way that there's a fine line between confidence and arrogance. Being a bully is far easier than being an alpha male so, in this chapter, you'll learn how to distinguish between the two and how to not be a bully.

Let's start with the example of two guys who work at the same place, say in middle management in some company. Both the guys seem confident and in control, but only one of them is an alpha male. The other is simply a bully. But how do we tell the difference? What if the bully thinks of himself as an alpha male without realizing that he is actually a bully? Should we even care for the difference?

Yes, we should. It's important for a number of reasons, the first one being that alpha males almost always get the most desirable women. It may not seem like such an important thing to some of you, but trust me, in the path of life, it *is* an important thing. Women actively look for alpha men, not just for fun, but also for long-lasting relationships. And when you're in for a long haul, you can't convince your partner to stay with you unless you're a true alpha male. Bullies may succeed for a while but soon mess up and show their true colors. That's when the women leave them to find real alpha males.

But if that doesn't convince you, there's another reason. Alpha males are the real deal; they're the real leaders. Bullies are usually just cowards who pull up a façade of aggression to hide their cowardice. They *create* problems! Alpha men, on the other hand, are problem-solvers. So from a professional point of view, which one out of the two is more likely to get a promotion?

These two reasons are more than enough to convince you that distinguishing yourself from bullies, as a true alpha, is important. So let's discoverer what makes an alpha male what he is?

What Makes an Alpha Male?

A researcher once asked Joe Montana about his game, trying to understand what goes on in his mind when he plays. "Do you see the ball, take a step forward, and then throw it?"

Montana's answer was quite different from what the researcher expected. According to him, it was all one thing for him and there was no separation between the various actions. He even said that he did most of it without being fully aware of it.

And that's how it is for alpha males moving through life. When they encounter a situation, they quickly make an assessment and take the most logical step, based on their experience. They're confident that it will work, and there's no separation between the various steps. It's all one thing: observation-action-outcome.

What Makes a Bully?

Bullies often give the impression of being alpha males. They come off as assertive and decisive; they get things done on their own terms and are not afraid to express themselves. They seem confident when they go against someone, not at all afraid, but there's a key difference between bullies and alpha males. Bullies only go up against people whom they know they can dominate.

That is why it can be difficult to discern them from true alpha males. They seem energetic and decisive enough, and they *want* to be thought of as alpha males, but they are not really.

How Do You Differentiate?

One of the best and fastest ways to see the difference is to watch how people tackle opposition. An alpha male stays cool and pays attention to things going on while taking on the opposition. He is alert and knows how to make things go his way without being overly aggressive. He knows how he can influence the world around him by seizing the opportunities whenever they present themselves. Once an alpha male starts toward a goal, the thought of failure doesn't occur to him, and he does things naturally. He doesn't give up easily and keeps trying while constantly assessing the situation to get what he wants. This is not to say that an alpha male never makes a mistake. He most certainly can and does, but he has a way of dealing with it.

He takes note of what he should've done instead, and then moves on, learning the right lessons. He doesn't mull over his mistake for too long, and he doesn't mope. He sees life as an endless stream of opportunities for success. An alpha male loves winning, and is also good at it.

When an alpha male makes a mistake, he doesn't beat himself up about it unnecessarily. Unlike bullies, his public image doesn't matter to him so much. He simply cares about the right thing to do, and that's what he learns from the mistake. So he doesn't waste his time mulling over the mistake over and over.

Another thing to note is that a bully rarely ever goes against someone bigger and stronger than him. And when we say "bigger" and "stronger," it isn't always about the physical attributes of the other person. It can also be used figuratively, talking about the other person's strength of character and spirit. A bully always goes for a soft target, and enjoys having a large audience as he attacks his target.

The term "grandstander" fits right for bullies. They are conscious of how they look when they're doing anything, and they love having people around to see them vanquish their opponent. They have aggression on their faces, but inside, they're actually scared. That is why they shrink away, afraid, whenever someone who is actually strong challenges them.

Alpha males are on the other end of the spectrum in this regard. They are hardly ever self-conscious, not caring about how they look to other people. An alpha male would much rather direct his energy toward solving the problem at hand and getting the job done. They get stuff done and then move on, and that is the source of their confidence.

If we compare alpha males in humans to alpha males in wolves, we can find a lot of similarities. Both of them share important qualities. Just as in a wolf pack, a human alpha male is a natural leader, protective of his pack (partner, friends, teammates, family), self-confident, and extremely loyal. They are sure of themselves and know how to handle anything thrown their way. More often than not, they are physically fit, and they also tend to stay low-key until they are needed. They never relinquish control to someone else and keep some part of themselves independent, even in the army and other similar professions. And, most important, alpha males are true leaders.

In conclusion, an alpha male is smart, strong, and a pack builder. He leads with confidence, and does everything to protect and provide for his pack. And, most important, he has *fun* doing it all.

CHAPTER 17

DEALING WITH THE ALPHA MALE

You will come across alpha males everywhere. At your workplace, home, friend circle, anywhere. They are domineering, arrogant, intimidating, and impatient with details and people. They are best sustained in an atmosphere thriving with responsibility and action and drive. So, how do you deal with such people in general? Read on to find out.

1. Take a stand: Do not get swayed by their opinions and arguments. You also have a right to speak up and put your points forward. If you believe in something strongly, go on and say it.

2. Speak their language: Alpha males delight in pointing out the mistakes of others. It makes them feel rather invincible. Instead of feeling angry or ashamed of your mistake, get back to them in their own language. For example, if he tells you, "You're wrong," ask him, "How do you make it right?" The message will be understood, loud and clear.

3. Never compromise on your dignity: Your self-respect is entirely in your hands. The leader of the pack is not here to look out for you and your best interests. He is not interested in you as a person nor does he value your opinion. If you let him get to you, you stand the chance of being exposed by him, especially your weaknesses. Maintain your integrity at all costs.

4. Use your EQ: Of all your capacities; you will need the maximum amount of your emotional quotient to deal with alphas. They are majorly result-oriented; they will undoubtedly trample upon people and egos. You will inevitably be judged on how good or useful you are. Do not let him get to you. Deal with the criticism in a mature manner. Don't take it personally.

5. Be direct: Beating around the bush, hemming and hawing around, and evasiveness will rub him the wrong way. Be analytical, direct, and logical. Feelings and emotions should take a back seat when conversing with him. Present him with data, facts, and logic and win him over.

6. Learn to be thick-skinned: Being overly sensitive will get you nowhere. The alpha will barely notice you or your emotions and the effect of his words on your psyche. He couldn't care less. Do not let him get to you at all.

7. Stay neutral: If you want to get along with an alpha, refrain from expressing your weak points. Even a simple statement like "I'm learning the ropes" or "I have a long way to go" can be easily misconstrued by him. Just go with the flow. Sentences like "I hear you" or "It won't happen again" are a safer bet.

8. Avoid appearing submissive: If you show the slightest hint of submissiveness, you will lose his respect. His anger might scare you, but don't let it show. He is doing that to please his ego, not hurt yours. Just be cool and collected.

Dealing with Alpha Males in the Workplace

- Ladies, please do not try to outdo an alpha male. At least, appear not to. The alpha likes women to act like women, not like his own ilk. For all your strength, stamina, superior mental faculties, and multitasking ability, the alpha male will feel threatened if he sees a woman who is much better than him. Just leave him be.

- Expect a major and ugly fight every time you want to subdue or conquer the alpha male. As long as he is within his limits with regards to the discussion or issue at hand, it's fine. The minute he gets offensive, don't be afraid of challenging him. Do so in a calm manner, not in an agitated way, which will further instigate him.

- The modern alpha man is a throwback to the early man of yore, who needed to impress the females of the group with his hunting and carving skills. He needs women to be awed by his awesome power, status, and decision-making abilities. Keep this is mind when he starts strutting about.

- But refrain from getting swayed by his charm and manner. If the alpha begins to sense that the people around him are easily mesmerized by him or hang on to his every word, he quickly loses interest. Genuine admiration is different from ass kissing. As reiterated, keep your dignity intact.

- You might see your alpha boss or manager give themselves personal challenges to meet and goals to accomplish. They need this kind of competitiveness around where they can pit their wits against their opponents and come up trumps. Though males have a general idea about how other males will behave in a combative situation, they are totally clueless when it comes to dealing with a female perspective.

- To do that, don't beat around the bush. Be direct, clear, and concise. Loud, rambling arguments will not bode well for you. Your sentences should be clearly thought out and no unnecessary pauses should punctuate them. Make sure you sound convincing.

- No unnecessary apologies, please! Do not keep saying "sorry" or "I apologize" for no reason at all.

Phrases like "I'm afraid I have to" or "I really hope you don't mind" or "Sorry to bother you" should be weeded out at all costs when dealing with an alpha. Go out directly and ask what you want to.

- When talking, watch your tone. Don't go all soft or whisper your words. Faltering, whining, speaking too slowly, or using sentences with too many pauses displays your nervousness and uncertainty. Even if your intentions are right, you will come across as a pushover and you are more likely to be ignored.

- Your body language communicates a lot more about you than your words ever will. Slouching, shuffling, refusing eye contact, a weak handshake, shifting your weight, etc., all make you look more submissive and passive than you actually are. Stand up straight, look at people in the eye, speak in a clear voice, and get your point across.

- Learn to say no: People often accept unwanted assignments or do things that they'd rather not do just to maintain cordiality among relations and not hurt the other person. Alphas do not recognize any such niceties. If you think you are not up for a certain task, be bold and say no. Offer sound reason and logic behind your decision. Do not be afraid to assert yourself. This is a learned skill. If you don't treat yourself with respect, nobody around you will either. It's all in your hands. Don't let others take advantage of you.

CHAPTER 18

THE DOWNSIDE OF BEING ALPHA

All those who do not want to be an alpha male, raise your hands. What? None? No one? Obviously. Which guy doesn't want to be an alpha? Alphas get whatever they want. The best women, the best things in life, and all the money and status.

But wait. According to a Princeton University study, there is a price to pay for that awesomeness. What price, you ask? Well, read on to find out.

This study was conducted with a 125 baboons, yes, another of our closest relatives, over a period of ten years, and was released in the *Science Journal.* What it found was that being the alpha male of the pack is extremely stressful. The baboons at the top of the hierarchy had the maximum levels of testosterone and glucocorticoid, the stress hormones. Not feeling so cocky now, eh? Furthermore, the study focused on some other aspects of being the alpha male. In order to protect their position, the top male had the additional strain of fending off other animals in the pack and, in general, keeping himself in fighting fit condition to protect the females in the group and provide for the troops. The onus of the responsibility of the entire pack fell on the alpha male's shoulders. Another interesting fact that came to light was that the omegas too exhibited the same stress levels as the alphas. The betas apparently had an easy ride. Their stress levels were considerably low.

Evolutionary History

Now, let's go back to our roots. Our evolutionary history. Darwin's theory of natural selection was a big hit many years after it had been proposed. It was only a matter of time before this theory came to be applied to psychological phenomena as well. The idea that, if human beings were displaying a certain behavior trait or characteristic, it must be a genetically advantageous trait; because, if it weren't, the trait would've vanished or died out with time. Only the strongest genes and traits survive.

Case in point: The innate fear of snakes, spiders, worms. If we go by research, it suggests that this fear is innate. Despite the overwhelming evidence that deaths due to snakebites occur with extreme rarity in nature, people all over the world list snakes as their number one fear. The argument goes that this fear is advantageous to survival, since snakes are perceived as poisonous, although only an exceedingly small percentage of the snake population is deadly. Therefore, a large number of people display this trait.

If we go on to the topic at hand, one may claim that, from a biological viewpoint, all women are attracted toward dominant and socially superior males. There is a strong reasoning behind this. In biological terms, it is the woman who has to carry the offspring to term, bear the horrendous pain of childbirth, and spend many months caring for the child. It is only natural that she seeks out the most powerful, strong, good-looking, rich, and socially superior male who can provide her and her future children with the safety, comfort, and love that she craves. Therefore, the argument goes, women tend to lean toward the dominant and powerful male.

Monogamy is another example. In evolutionary terms, the male who spread his sperm around and fathered the maximum number of children had the greatest chances at propagating his line, therefore implying that natural selection favors promiscuity. Human beings, despite the constraints and barriers put before them in the form of relationships like marriage, still cheat on each other and practice promiscuity. Alpha males tend to be more promiscuous than the betas and omegas for obvious reasons. They do have more chances of passing on their genes. Therefore, as far as evolutionary biology goes, being non-monogamous is advantageous over monogamy. As you may have seen in your friend circles or heard about from others, there are lots of ways to have polyamory. If you are in a couple situation already, it does not mean you are stuck necessarily. Couples sometimes decide together to bring flexibility or openness to their relationships. This can mean bringing new sexual partners into the bedroom from time to time. This might also mean establishing certain rules that allow each partner to engage with others.

Obviously, health as well as pregnancy are things to manage, but more and more couples are considering this lifestyle. It is not full-out swinging (although that is an option too) but it is a perhaps safer and more manageable middle ground. Trust, communication, and boundaries are critical to making it work. It is doable. Again, think of using power, not force when raising this with your partner. Have it be something you generate together. Listen to their concerns and look for solutions. This is a much bolder approach than cheating and trying to uphold a string of lies.

Alpha Male

CONCLUSION

Phew! Enough with these alphas and betas and omegas, right? But just look around you. Look at the animals. The animal kingdom is a pretty harsh and unforgiving place to live in. The alpha males in each animal species, be it the lion or the tiger or the gorilla or the wolf, have it much rougher than humans. They are forced to fight to the death, have bloody and macabre dragged-out sessions, just to claim the title of the alpha male. But ah, victory is sweet. After the fight, after the dust has settled and the competitors vanquished, the winner just sits back, while the females surround him and tend to his wounds and look after him. It's good to be at the top, eh?

This is natural selection at play. Darwin got it spot on when he said that nature favors the strongest and the fastest. This is nature's way of ensuring that only the strongest animals survive. These alphas will, in turn, spread their seed far and wide, thus making sure that their lineage never dies out. But there is a cruel twist of nature. The very same alpha is one day taken down by his progeny.

Okay, well, we are humans. We have evolved after thousands of years and possess a fully functioning brain and lots of conditioning throughout childhood that aids our decision-making processes. We operate in a much more complex social structure, with barriers and relationships and lines joining the two. Our ability to think, empathize, and reason is unparalleled and this is the prime reason we are a civilized race. Killing is not a sport for us. But, as always, there is a limit to the evolutionary activity. Each of us still has some animal instinct within him or her, which occasionally comes to the fore when loved ones are threatened or when we see someone being attacked viciously. Human males might be relics of the ancient past, but they still want to be at the top of the hierarchy. And females still want to be seen with the most successful and handsome guy, not a loser fellow with long hair and a guitar in his hand.

Now, in the modern-day context, what does being an alpha truly entail? Is it the burly, hairy, scary-looking guy at the bar who keeps flexing his muscles, just itching for a fight? Or is it that spray-tanned beefy guy at the business dinner, complete with his gold Rolex and a diamond-tipped pen? How about a cocky, arrogant douche that is at the heart of every argument and just has to make his point the best one? Are all these alphas? Sadly, no. We know it, they know it. This kind of blatant display of wealth, success, machismo, and power might go down well among gorillas, but let's face it, in the real world; such people are shunned by society. No one wants to hang out with such a bore. So, who are we talking about here?

A true alpha does not have to prove anything to anybody. Watch one in action. He will be the one whom everyone looks up to. Someone who doesn't pick fights voluntarily, yet does not back down from them. Someone who holds his ground till the end of the battle. He doesn't go on and on about his conquests or wealth or the number of business deals he has clinched. He has class and knows how to display it just so. Alphas do not throw their tongues around. They know exactly what attracts women to them, and it's not all about money. A true alpha is super confident in his skin, subtly powerful, cool, calm, and collected in all situations. No showing off at all. They know people will be attracted to their personalities.

Alphas are natural leaders. In fact, all of us, whether we admit it or not, are drawn to someone who can lead us as a cohesive group. Leaders are charismatic people who keep the group as one. This kind of confidence which alphas have gives them extra inner strength to work with, which is all the more irresistible.

Now that you've learned about what being an alpha male is and how to become one, it's time to move forward by doing two things: Apply what you learned and read up more on the components that make for being alpha. Knowledge is useless without application and merely reading this e-book doesn't make you anymore alpha than reading a recipe book makes you a chef. If knowing is half the battle, then application of what you learned is the other half.

So you're not an alpha male but dying to be one. Simple. Look deep within yourself. What are your strengths? What inspires confidence in you? What is it that you do best? Find answers to these questions and start utilizing them to build your inner alpha. Train your strengths to become your guardian angels. Find your inner strength and slowly, you'll find people around you giving you more and more respect. Learn to love and respect yourself, no one else will do it for you. Then sit back and watch the world follow you.

As you've read throughout this book thus far, it really is about living an authentic life. It's about being unapologetic about being yourself. It is about being fully self-expressed. You are good enough. And don't forget the rule "fake it until you make it." That holds up. If you feel like you're not quite the part yet, don't fret. There is often a little homework to do. The only thing is to find a way to set aside any self-doubt and just be out there as proud as you can be about you. Conjure up your character strengths and your ability to connect with others. You do not need to be the smartest, fittest or wealthiest in the room. Being the alpha is about expressing who you are without crafting your image. You have to just go for it. Be connected to others. Be the life of the party. Give and take at the highest level. Don't hold back from living to the fullest.

Confidence is your friend. It is most important that you go ahead and be perfectly fine about everything you are and everything you aren't. Don't try to hide things or project a certain persona. Just be you. Anything that others wouldn't like is just fine from this perspective. You manage to still draw in friends, women, and admirers. You just "be" and don't spend so much time thinking about "doing." Be bold. Be confident. Be alpha. That's all. There is nothing more you need to do. You don't need to wait until you feel ready. The time is now. The more you get into the natural persona of being an alpha, the more you live in that space. You become comfortable in your own skin. Whatever comes up is irrelevant. You can handle it. You keep your cool. You make things better. You stand for things. You matter.

As you start applying what you learned, I'm excited for the transformations that will happen in your life on your way to experiencing life to the full by becoming legendary – a lion among sheep, an alpha male.

Here's to your successful transformation! Cheers!